SLOWING DOWN THE OUR FATHER

Slowing Down the Our Father

Leonard Foley, O.F.M.

Nihil Obstat: Rev. Hilarion Kistner, O.F.M.
Rev. John J. Jennings

Imprimi Potest: Rev. Jeremy Harrington, O.F.M.
Provincial

Imprimatur: +James H. Garland, V.G.
Archdiocese of Cincinnati
December 10, 1985

The *nihil obstat* and *imprimatur* are a declaration that a book or pamphlet is considered to be free from doctrinal or moral error. It is not implied that those who have granted the *nihil obstat* and *imprimatur* agree with the contents, opinions or statements expressed.

Unless otherwise indicated, all Scripture texts used in this work are taken from the *New American Bible,* copyright © 1970 by the Confraternity of Christian Doctrine, Inc., Washington, D.C., and are used by permission of the copyright owner. All rights reserved.

Book design and cover by Julie Lonneman.

SBN 0-89716-075-6

© 1986, Leonard Foley, O.F.M.
All rights reserved.
Published by St. Anthony Messenger Press.
Printed in the U.S.A.

Contents

I
Our Father Who Art in Heaven
11

II
Hallowed Be Thy Name
23

III
Thy Kingdom Come
35

IV
Thy Will Be Done on Earth as It Is in Heaven
43

V
Give Us This Day Our Daily Bread
59

VI
And Forgive Us Our Trespasses as We Forgive Those Who Trespass Against Us
69

VII
And Lead Us Not Into Temptation But Deliver Us From Evil
83

VIII
For Thine Is the Kingdom and the Power and the Glory Forever and Ever. Amen.
95

Introduction

"*I don't pray very well!*" Many of us today are lamenting that fact that we "can't" pray. Perhaps it's the crazy times, we say: high speed and high tech, noisy traffic and noisy music, the overload of sight and sound, the constant adoration around the TV altar, the rush and hurry and split-second scheduling.

Or maybe we're just lazy. The Bomb hasn't gone off yet, and we Americans (not counting the poor) are living in the most comfortable, overfed, gadget-filled, unchallenging environment of all time. Has God become the repairman who's never needed?

Or perhaps the "changes" in the Church have left us insecure, afraid we'll miss the latest "in" thing in spirituality. Should we put all our eggs in the charismatic basket, or are the Latin Mass people right after all? As Yoga and Zen and psychology set up stand in church, can we afford to rely on those old meditation books? We are vaguely dissatisfied with prayer books with "canned" prayers, and, sadly enough, the rosary takes too long for our jumpy society.

Or maybe we are ignoring Jesus' instructions not to "rattle on like the pagans." We were taught, and teach our children, to *recite* prayers, which of course is not the same as praying. We are fascinated with memorization. Little

Johnny *knows* the Our Father and Hail Mary. Does he? We *recite* meal prayers eyeing the pork chops (though some of the meandering "spontaneous" meal prayers are no better).

Listen to the congregation at your church some Sunday, booming through the Gloria and the Creed with a speed that would do justice to a tobacco auctioneer. We are the generation of the jet and the thundering stereos. We dread silence and slowness.

Things are not totally bad, of course. The very people who say they "can't" pray, actually *do* pray—and very well. If you ask them whether they "talk to God" during the day, the answer is usually, "Oh, sure!" In spite of the crashing culture around them, they maintain a closeness, even an intimacy, with God, Jesus, the Spirit. (Mothers of small children seem to fall into this category in especially high numbers.)

This book is meant to help these ordinary people have a little better awareness of the God they talk to, and of the Son who revealed him, and of the Spirit who lives in them. What better place to start, if we are to continue the struggle to pray, than with the *Lord's* prayer?

Those of us who live in a Christian country may forget that this is the prayer that distinguishes Christians from all other pray-ers. In Luke's Gospel we learn that when Jesus' followers saw that John the Baptist had taught *his* disciples a special prayer, they asked Jesus to give them a prayer that would be theirs alone (cf. Luke 11:1). So Jesus taught them the Our Father. It's not, then, just a universal prayer, though anyone can pray it. Christians pray this prayer with all the peace and pain of the Gospels pressing upon their minds and hearts.

In Matthew's Gospel, however, a different reason is given for Jesus' teaching the Our Father. The prayer is found in the Sermon on the Mount, and Jesus has just cautioned against praying like the hypocrites, who "love to stand and pray in synagogues or on street corners in order to be noticed" (Matthew 6:5). He has told them not to "rattle on like the pagans. They think they will win a hearing by the sheer multiplication of words. Do not imitate them. Your Father knows what you need before you ask him" (6:7-8).

Jesus is almost saying that words aren't really all that important—at least not for God, who knows all about it before we start. *We*, however, may need a long time and a long prayer to get our own heads and hearts straight.

In contrast to the prayer of the show-offs and the rattlers, then, Jesus gives us a simple way of communing with God. The prayer rests like a jewel almost at the center of the Sermon on the Mount: surrounded by Jesus' words about salt and light, purity of body and spirit and intention, anger and reconciliation, fasting and bearing fruit, the Golden Rule and the house built on rock.

The spirit of the Gospel resonates in the Our Father. It is a prayer for the followers of Jesus.

Two Our Fathers?

Only two of the four Gospels give us the Our Father: Matthew and Luke. It is interesting to compare the two versions (in three translations); see the chart on pp. 4-5.

First of all, notice the differences between these translations and the Our Father we grew up reciting. Throughout this book the chapter headings draw upon the words of this traditional Our Father which we still pray at liturgy. The three translations* referred to throughout the text appear on the facing page at each chapter's beginning. Comparing and contrasting these various Our Fathers will

---

*The *New American Bible* (NAB) is a translation by members of the Catholic Biblical Association of America, and sponsored by the Bishops' Committee of the Confraternity of Christian Doctrine. It was published in 1970.

The *Jerusalem Bible* (JB) was originally a French translation by the Dominican Biblical School in Jerusalem in 1956. The English version (1966) is not a translation from the French, but from the original Hebrew and Greek. One of the great values of this book is the extensive notes and introductions translated from the French.

The *Revised Standard Version* (RSV) is the latest of several revisions of the *King James Version* published in 1611. Publication began in 1952, and a final New Testament revision was published in 1971.

be one way of exploring the richness of the prayer Jesus taught us.

Second, what about the two *versions* in Scripture?

Scholars generally hold that Luke's version more closely represents—in the number of its petitions—the *form* of the prayer as historically spoken by Jesus. The simple reason for this position is that it is hardly probable that anyone or any community would have dared to remove

---

Matthew 6:9-13　　　　　　*Luke 11:2-4*

New American Bible

Our Father in heaven,	Father,
hallowed be your name,	hallowed be your name,
your kingdom come,	your kingdom come.
your will be done	
on earth as it is in heaven.	
Give us today our daily bread,	Give us each day our daily bread.
and forgive us the wrong we have done	Forgive us our sins
as we forgive those who wrong us.	for we too forgive all who do us wrong;
Subject us not to the trial but deliver us from the evil one.	and subject us not to the trial.

Jerusalem Bible

Our Father in heaven,	Father,
may your name be held holy,	may your name be held holy,
your kingdom come,	your kingdom come;
your will be done,	
on earth as in heaven.	

any petition attributed to Jesus. But the two petitions in Matthew which are not found in Luke do have parallels in the Gospels. A common explanation of the "expansion" of Matthew is that it happened under the influence of liturgy. We must remember that for a while there was nothing written—Gospels, "Mass books," lectionaries, etc. Almost certainly the words that were used for the Eucharist were slightly different in different areas, though retaining

---

Give us today our daily bread.
And forgive us our debts, as we have forgiven those who are in debt to us.
And do not put us to the test,
but save us from the evil one.

give us each day our daily bread,
and forgive us our sins, for we ourselves forgive each one who is in debt to us.
And do not put us to the test.

Revised Standard Version

Our Father who art in heaven,
Hallowed be thy name.
Thy kingdom come,
Thy will be done,
On earth as it is in heaven.
Give us this day our daily bread;
And forgive us our debts, As we also have forgiven our debtors;

And lead us not into temptation,
But deliver us from evil.

Father,
hallowed be thy name.
Thy kingdom come.

Give us each day our daily bread;
and forgive us our sins, for we ourselves forgive everyone who is indebted to us;
and lead us not into temptation.

basically what Jesus said. Hence the difference in Matthew and Luke.

The influence of different areas can be seen when the two versions are translated back into Aramaic, the language Jesus spoke. Scholars find a carefully crafted structure in each version. Matthew (who likes fives) has five statements of two lines each, with each line having two stresses. This was a meter familiar to the Old Testament and is believed to show a kind of Aramaic spoken in Jesus' own Galilee. Luke, on the other hand, translates back into seven phrases of seven syllables each. The Aramaic here is thought to have been common in other parts of Palestine (that is, outside of Galilee). This form was also well known.

The fact that we have these two versions set forth without embarrassment in the New Testament shows how little the early Christians were affected by the legalism and formalism that Jesus denounced throughout the Gospels. Jesus was giving us a *model* for Christian prayer. He gave us the prayer substantially, but not exactly. And surely he repeated his instructions many times, very probably not always in the same words.

The greatest difference between the two versions in Matthew and Luke has to do with their respective outlooks on the future. The famous American Bible scholar Raymond Brown, in a long article in *Theological Studies*, explains a position that is fairly common among scholars: that the Our Father in Matthew is an *eschatological* prayer (or, for those who don't like mystic-sounding foreign words, an *end-time* prayer). "By 'eschatological,'" Father Brown says, "we refer to the period of the last days, involving the return of Christ, the destruction of the forces of evil, and the definite establishment of God's rule."

Matthew's community, in this opinion, was expecting *and praying for* the imminent return of Jesus. The prayer asks that God's name be hallowed, his will done, the eternal banquet given, the Evil One destroyed, etc.—*once and for all*. Scholars come to this conclusion because certain word forms in Matthew's original language have precisely that emphasis: *once and for all, definitively*.

Luke's version, on the other hand, has a different emphasis. Notice the difference between Matthew's petition—"Give us *today* our daily bread"—and Luke's: "Give us *each day* our daily bread"—that is, one day after another into the indefinite future.

The usual explanation for this different emphasis is that, in Luke's community, what had once been an intense desire for the end-time now began to fade as time went on and Jesus did not return. Indeed, Luke's Gospel is credited with expressing the realization that the presence of the Spirit was the presence of the "absent" Jesus. As Father Brown puts it, the expectation of the imminent coming of Jesus "has begun to yield to the hard facts of daily Christian living." Christians must constantly be watchful, as Jesus repeatedly warned, but they must also follow the injunction of the two angels at the scene of Jesus' ascension, not to stand there "looking up at the skies" (Acts 1:11).

We of the Church today are similar to Luke's community in our outlook on the future. But, as Father Brown says, "as we say the prayer 19 centuries later, now completely enmeshed in the temporal aspects of the Christian life, it would perhaps profit us to revive in part some of the original eschatological yearning....The return of Christ comes closer every day."

Slowing Down the Our Father

To experience anew the Our Father's eschatological yearning, as well as to come to a fuller experience of the way the gospel message resonates in its every phrase, we need to slow this prayer down.

The epitome of "slowing down" is captured in a story that was a staple of the old parish missions: There was a woman who had been bedridden for many years. She always had a rosary in her hand, but it never moved. A fussy person noticed this and inquired why she never "got anyplace" with her rosary. The sick woman didn't answer, being humble. But later, to an intimate friend, she confided, "I never get past those first two words, 'Our Father.' I just hold them in my heart. I never feel like going on."

Most of us do feel like going on, as quickly as possible. But only by letting each word, each phrase, resonate in us can the Our Father's true power impress itself on us. The following reflections are offered to help slow down our *reciting* and transform it to *praying*.

Matthew 6:9	*Luke 11:2*
Our Father in heaven, (NAB, JB)	Father, (NAB, JB, RSV)
Our Father who art in heaven, (RSV)	

I

'OUR FATHER, WHO ART IN HEAVEN'

Little Arab children have a word for their mothers and fathers which sounds a lot like Jesus' word for his Father. They say *Jah-bah;* he said *Ab-ba* with the same soft *a* sound in Aramaic. And that one word is the first prayer he taught us.

Maybe there's something common to all babies of all time that makes their first "language" come out like "Ma-ma" or "Ba-ba" or "Da-da." The baby words carry over into childhood. In our country they become "Mom" or "Mama" or "Dad" or "Daddy."

We can't really say "Daddy" to God. The word has too many frivolous connotations besides its genuine meaning. But if we translate it back into a child's simple "Ba-ba" or "Ma-ma" or "Ab-ba," we will come close to Jesus' meaning when he gave us the Our Father in his native language.

Daring to Say 'Abba'

We who are so used to saying "Father" will probably not be able to understand what an amazing thing Jesus did in telling us to call God our Father by using the child's word "Abba."

For some reason, the Church did not insert "Abba"

as a translation of "Father" in the Our Father, as it did in a few other places in the New Testament (cf. Romans 8:15 and Galatians 4:6). The only other place in the Gospels where the word *Abba* is used (with "Father" in parentheses) is in Mark's account of Jesus' agony in the garden: "He kept saying, '*Abba* (O Father), you have the power to do all things. Take this cup away from me'" (14:36).

Here we see the poignancy of the word—something for us to remember as we say the Our Father. Jesus is expressing his simple, trusting, childlike spirit. When he cried out, "Abba!" he was being his true human self— totally Father-centered and God-dependent. It is this child's intimacy that he teaches us first. "Abba, good Father, our God and our all!" There is no need to hurry on. Savoring the one word can be our whole prayer, in time and in content. And if we, like the sick woman in the story in the Introduction (see p. 7), never "get past" that word we will be fortunate indeed.

"*Abba*." Imagine Jesus praying the word, and remember the trusting "Ma-ma's" and "Da-da's" you once said or have heard. At the raising of Lazarus: "Abba, I thank you for having heard me. I know that you always hear me" (John 11:41-42). Another time at prayer: "Abba, Lord of heaven and earth, to you I offer praise; for what you have hidden from the learned and the clever you have revealed to the merest children" (Matthew 11:25). And then the three great "Abba's" of Jesus' confrontation with death: "Abba, if it is your will, take this cup from me; yet not my will but yours be done" (Luke 22:42); "Abba, forgive them; they do not know what they are doing" (23:24); "Abba, into your hands I commend my spirit" (23:46).

Jesus was truly and completely human, as mature as humanity can be. But he did not "outgrow" childhood before the Father. He was always totally secure in the nearness of his Father.

It took Jesus' followers a while to get used to the expression "Abba." As noted above, the word *Abba* is found in only one place in the four Gospels—Mark 14:36.

Paul probably put exclamation points all over the

paragraph in his letter to the Church in Galatia when he reminded them that they were not slaves, but *children* of God. Without any disrespect, they could talk to God like little children, saying "Da-da." They might still use formal and stately religious language ("Almighty and eternal God," "Lord, God of heaven and earth"), but when they said *their* special Christian prayer, they should say "Abba!"

The proof that they are children, and dare address God this way, Paul says, is the fact that God has "sent forth into our hearts the Spirit of his Son which cries out, 'Abba!'" Because Gentiles might not know this Aramaic word, he translated it: "Father" (Galatians 4:1-7). And he told the Romans that they had not received a "slave" spirit, but rather one of adoption, through which they could cry out, "Abba!" (Romans 8:15).

Luke's version of the Our Father simply begins with the one word "Father" (again, "Abba" in the original). But Matthew feels obliged to put a stately setting around the jewel: He puts "Our" before and "who art in heaven" after. Jesus may have taught several versions of the prayer, of course, and the liturgical use of the prayer by the Christians for whom Matthew wrote (probably both Jews and Gentiles, at Antioch) may have required the expansion. (It may have been easier, for instance, to sing the long phrase.) But it's a good bet that "Abba" was threateningly intimate at first and, perhaps, was not widely used. Was a far-off God "safer" for these early Christians? For us? Would intimacy demand too much? Does it, for us?

The risks of intimacy with the Father, however, fade in comparison with the rewards. There is no one on earth as accessible as our Father. We may have gotten so used to this fact that we take it too much for granted. The best human fathers must sometimes retreat into their own privacy, but "Abba!" is a *direct line* 24 hours a day. Actually God always calls us first; or, rather, the line is always open. The Father is someone with a heart to talk to. And if "heart speaks to heart," in the happy phrase of Cardinal Newman, and we never "get past" the opening words, "Our Father," "Abba," both hearts are satisfied.

'My Father and Your Father'

The daring intimacy with which Jesus taught us to call upon his father does not imply that we relate to the Father in exactly the same way as Jesus. There is a sense in which Jesus cannot really say "our" with us. He is the eternal Son of God, the unique, only-begotten One, equal to the Father, one in nature. We are created beings. Our grace is to share the life of the Father insofar as a creature can accept the divine. The Son of God's grace is his nature. He is Son of God by right, eternally, naturally. We are children by gift, by a freely given sharing that is more than human adoption but infinitely less than the Sonship by right of the Second Person of the Trinity.

Therefore we can understand Jesus' saying, "I am ascending to my Father and your Father, to my God and your God!" (John 20:17). The Gospels, written in the light of the Resurrection and the awareness of Jesus' divinity, are careful to record that Jesus said "my Father" 47 times but used the phrase "our Father" only once, when he tells *us* how to pray. "This is how you are to pray: 'Our Father...'" (Matthew 6:9).

This distinction has to be made because it is true, but we needn't go overboard. Jesus is also a truly human being, and as such he is as dependent on the Father as we are. His human nature is graced with childhood in a way similar to ours. We can imagine him, when he sees the crowds being baptized by John, entering the water with them, putting his arms around them and praying, "Abba, Our Father!" It is the amazing mystery of the Incarnation that one who could say "my Father" as equal Son also came to say "our Father" in a created human nature. He came to make us sons and daughters in the same way that he was a human son—totally graced and totally dependent. And until we see the mystery of heaven, it is better that we keep him on the human side.

The Prayer of the People of Jesus

Anyone can say the Our Father, but Jesus taught it as the "official" prayer of *his* people. One day the apostles, noting that John the Baptist had given a distinctive way of praying to his followers, asked Jesus (maybe wanting to keep up with the Joneses) to give them a special way of praying as *his* followers. It was then that Jesus taught his friends the Our Father.

There is no snobbishness in Christians' claiming this prayer as their own. It is simply a fact that each family has its own unique experience and "story." No one else can say "Mother" or "Father" as the children of any particular family can say those words. Those who for whatever reason do not belong to Jesus' family can be compared, at least generally, to someone who finds a child's letter to a parent. The words are familiar, but the meaning of this particular child cannot even be guessed: All the experiences that mother or father and child have had are captured in the simple unshareable words. No other child can "copy" them.

Only after the climactic events of Jesus' death and resurrection and the coming of the Spirit could Jesus' friends (his "family" of brothers and sisters) begin to suspect the full meaning of his words and life. They came to see that the Our Father was the center of the Sermon on the Mount and reflected the ultimate meaning of *Jesus'* unique teaching. It's a nice prayer in itself, but only those who know Jesus can know its "Jesus" meaning.

So the Our Father is the prayer of Jesus' community, which itself is formed by saying the prayer in faith, hope and love. It is the prayer of those who know the risen Savior.

Called to Pray in Community

In the early Church the Our Father was said three times a day. And it was said only by those who were baptized. It wasn't printed in a million books: In fact, the candidates for baptism (catechumens) did not even know of the existence of the prayer until a certain stage of their preparation, when there was a solemn "revealing" and handing over of the prayer to them. Part of their becoming real members of the community was their being empowered to say this prayer! This is the practice recaptured in today's Rite of Christian Initiation for Adults.

Any individual Christian can say the prayer alone, of course, but it will be the prayer *Jesus* taught only if his other words are remembered: "This is how all will know you for my disciples; by your love for one another" (John 13:35).

No man is an island, and still less are Christians a lot of self-propelled individuals "saving" their souls by personal effort. They are a Body whose members are alive because they are members. As Paul might say, "Can an eye say to the hand, 'I can forget about you when I pray'? Or an ear say to the foot, 'Your prayers have nothing to do with mine'?"

The great spiritual writer Romano Guardini has noted that *by nature* I am a man among men, a woman among women. But *by grace* I am primarily a brother or sister—not in the general sense that all the world's a family—of Jesus and in Jesus, with a distinctive way of saying, "*Our* Father."

The Spirit of Jesus therefore calls us to pray as a choir, not as soloists. We pray not for *my* needs first, but for *ours*. "Go to your room" to pray as Jesus said (Matthew 6:6), but take your brothers and sisters along in your heart. It is only when we stand together that we "know who we are," as the modern phrase goes. God listens carefully to the prayer of every individual, but it is striking that Jesus said, "If two of you join your voices on earth to pray for anything whatever, it shall be granted you by my Father in heaven. Where two or three are gathered in my name, there am I in their midst" (Matthew 18:19-20).

But can't it ever be "I"? May it never be *my* prayer? Perhaps a good way of answering that question is to put it this way: We must go to the Father as members of the Body of Jesus; but the Father comes to us not only as community but also as particularly loved individual children. There can be no private way to the Father that ignores my brothers and sisters. But our gift from the Father is a special name: "To the victor I will give the hidden manna; I will also give him a white stone upon which is inscribed a new name, to be known only by him who receives it" (Revelation 2:17).

Each child has a special relationship to the father and to the mother. So it is with us. God addresses each one of us differently: We are not a list of numbers. God is always there *completely* for me (but not completely for *me*).

There is no duplicate in the world of the relationship I have with our Father. There is, as Guardini says, "an exclusiveness between us, a secret no one can enter." So we can humbly say with Mary, "God who is mighty has done great things for me" (Luke 1:49). I do not deserve the relationship, but I do have it, and it would simply be untrue to deny it.

Our 'New,' 'Real' Father

God does not change, but in a certain sense Jesus gave us a new image of the Father. God had always been the Father of his people, as covenant partner and protector. There are tender passages in the Old Testament which see God as never forgetting any of his children even if their mother might, and as gently lifting a baby to his cheek.

The "new" Father began to become evident with the death and resurrection of Jesus. It started to dawn on the little Church that, because Jesus was truly *the* Son as well as *a* son, he was *the* Son in a special way of One who is

Father in a special way. When he said he had come that we might have life, he meant a life that could only be begotten by the Father.

But weren't people sharing in this life begotten by the Father (that is, in the "state of grace") before Jesus, and weren't at least some of them intimately united to the Father whom Jesus revealed? Yes, of course. But we are people of history, and God can deal with us only along a line of years and centuries. There had to be a particular time when Jesus appeared as the definitive revelation of the Father. "I am the true Vine and my Father is the vinegrower" (John 15:1) simply could not have been spoken before the Vine began to grow on earth.

There is, thus, a Father that no one can know unless Jesus reveals him: "No one knows the Son but the Father, and no one knows the Father but the Son—and anyone to whom the Son wishes to reveal him" (Matthew 11:27). Through Jesus we meet the Father: "If you really knew me, you would know my Father also. From this point on you know him; you have seen him" (John 14:7).

In a sense everyone in the world is Jesus' brother or sister. But "whoever does the will of my heavenly Father is brother and sister and mother to me" (Matthew 12:50). Doing the will of the Father means obeying *the Father we see in Jesus*, not merely a general World Director. With the "new" Father we also know a "new" Spirit who could not really be known until seen as the Spirit of Jesus and of the Father.

God is not our Father in a way that is something like that of our earthly father; rather, earthly fathers at their best are something faintly like our heavenly Father. It is that Father who really "raises" us—giving us daily food, both material and spiritual—who protects and comforts us, embraces us, walks with us. He also "raises" us to his own level of life.

Jesus said it this way:

"Would one of you hand his son a stone when he asks for a loaf, or a poisonous snake when he asks for a fish? If you [parents, fathers], with all your sins, know how to give your children what is good, how much more will your heavenly Father give good things to anyone who asks him!"

(Matthew 7:19)

Luke's version is: "How much more will the heavenly Father give the Holy Spirit to those who ask him" (Luke 11:13). In other words, the best Father, the real Father, gives the best gifts, the real ones.

But isn't this restrictive? By saying that we have a "new" and "real" Father that can be known only in Jesus, aren't we taking away from the world at large the Father who holds it in his hand?

We are not excluding anyone. But again, Jesus is, in fact, *the* revelation of the Father, *the* way that Father chose to show us what kind of Father he is. Jesus said to Philip, "Whoever has seen me has seen the Father" (John 14:9). If some, through no fault of their own, do not know this, then we have the tremendous responsibility of making that Father known. But we cannot blur the difference between a God who is "deduced" by the human mind (and often in a distorted way) and the God of Jesus.

'Who Art in Heaven'

As we have seen, Luke simply puts a childlike "Abba," by itself, at the beginning of the Our Father. The Christians for whom Matthew wrote evidently felt this was a bit stark, or bold, and gradually put "Our" and "who art in heaven" with it.

We might say that while Luke emphasizes what theologians call the *immanent* (dwelling within, remaining) aspect of God, Matthew emphasizes his *transcendent* (literally, one who climbs beyond all limits) dimension. When we say "in heaven," we mean God in the inmost nature of his being, the inaccessible God. Matthew's emphasis is a corrective, if one is needed, to our making

God too much of a "pal," someone we may respect less for his being so accessible, so easygoing, so concerned with our daily lives. This is a correct image, but not the only one.

We must not make God into our own image. God is totally Other. Human instinct tells us that there is One infinitely holy, pure, calm—beyond all imagining, all demand. God transcends space and time and the vagaries of this transient planet. He is not locked into this moment of history, as we are. This prayer to the One "in heaven" takes us out of our low-ceiling earthly realm and takes us to where God dwells.

To say God is transcendent is not to make him remote. Rather, it helps us relax in his arms without making him *merely* a "nice" earthly father. It would be a poor God who could be defined in human ideas, "graven images."

For God is not anything we are. God cannot be located or limited to any place on earth, even though he breaks through sacramentally wherever the Body of Jesus gathers.

Jesus was not abolishing public worship when he told the Samaritan woman, "An hour is coming when you will worship the Father neither on this mountain [Gerizim, the Samaritans' holy place] nor in Jerusalem....An hour is coming, and is already here, when authentic worshipers will worship the Father in Spirit and truth" (John 4:21, 23). But he had to remind us that God is every place, any place in the world, for me, for us: in the lonesomeness of the night, on a noisy street, when we are lost in sin or despair, when we are at peace, when we are alienated from all the world.

God is not "up there" or "out there." God is simply *here*, totally accessible to me, yet equally accessible to anyone in the world, anywhere, anytime. We do not need to go to any *place* to find God. This, of course, could be used as an excuse for not going to a church except for the fact that God calls us together to be his family. We are not visible as Jesus' Body unless we are together as such.

The First Two Words Suffice

So we still haven't "got past" the first words of our prayer: "Our Father." The hundreds of words written here have not begun to plumb the depths. But perhaps they contain a glimmer of what prayer really means: letting our Father simply *be* for us, quietly, calmly. God knows that chidren have to run around and make noise and play. But even those children know that the real place to be, when they're hurt or tired or just full of childhood, is in their mother's or father's arms.

My little brother had to play alone in our backyard when I was at school. After his death at age six, my mother told me that every once in a while he would come, open the screen door, and make sure she was in the house. He didn't say anything; he didn't have to "get past" that assurance. He just went back outside and played, secure.

Abba,
good Father,
we come to you as your little children.
We say "Abba"
like children all over the world.
We want you to know
that we realize our true "home"
when you put your arms around us.
We leave behind our worldly wisdom and our "power."
We don't bring you our "achievements" and our "virtue."
We bring only ourselves,
knowing our need for you,
knowing the privilege of being loved
in such a fatherly/motherly way,
and knowing how safe we are when you hold us.

Matthew 6:9	*Luke 11:2*
hallowed be your name, (NAB)	Same
may your name be held holy, (JB)	Same
Hallowed be thy name. (RSV)	Same

II

'HALLOWED BE THY NAME'

For about 60 years at least—I can't speak for all history—American Catholic kids have been vigorously singsonging: "Our Father, wh'art in heaven, *hollowed* be thy name!" They happily trusted that there was something mysteriously wonderful about "hollowing" God's name. The only "hollows" they knew were "Happy" and "Sleepy." There was "Holloween," of course, but that had nothing to do with church. Maybe they (let's confess it, *we*) thought it had something to do with "hollowing out" God's name, like a giant tree trunk, so that more people could get inside. Or maybe we just hoped that God's name would be "hollered" far and wide, so that everybody would hear.

As for "name," well, that was a label they tied around newborn babies' wrists so their mothers wouldn't take the wrong one home. It might be John or Ralph or Lucinda or Melanie: The names didn't mean anything, except that they usually helped, later on, to tell the women-persons from the men-persons when there wasn't any other way to know who was what.

Sometimes names were given in parental admiration for movie stars, presidents, or as an honor to Grandpa or Grandma. So there are people still walking this earth who answer to "Elvis," "Norma Jean," "Delano," and even "NRA"! (Catholics are supposed to pick saints' names for their children, but that practice seems to have given way to choosing appellations that seem to have come from a Hollywood agent.)

So we may be starting with a double handicap when it comes to "hallowed be thy name": First, God's name may be just a label of three letters; second, none of us may remember ever hallowing anything at all.

The 'Name' of God

Names really are more than labels. The *way* a name is spoken is highly revealing. We don't start calling people by their first names right away (except in golf foursomes who just happen to coincide at the first tee). Why do husbands and wives and real friends never use "Mister" or "Miss" for each other (except in sarcasm)? What is the difference between "Helen" said quietly by a man who has been happily married to her for 40 years, and "Helen" said to a woman you meet for the first time at a PTA meeting? ("I'm Helen." "I'm Jack. Pleased to meet you, uh, Helen.") Or, finally, why did Mary Magdalen's heart suddenly burst for joy when the "gardener" of Gethsemane simply said, "Mary!"?

So, a name can throb with intimacy, or it can be a very formal means of address. In our relationship with God, both senses apply.

There's also something about a name that implies the ability to control on the part of the one who "knows" the name. A Bible scholar who had studied in the Holy Land once told me about a "name value" that still persists there. It's hard enough, he said, to get an Arab to allow a photograph. But when my friend once asked one of his photographees for his *name*—so he could send a copy—the man was horrified. "Oh no, no, no!" he said, "My name is *me!*" He meant, my friend said, that if you have my name you have some power over me; you know my personal secret, something intimate that I don't want you to have.

Another friend recalls the "superiority" he felt over

both his little brother and the animal they came upon in the woods. Its teeth were bared and his little brother was frightened. "Oh, that's just a little ole *possum*," my friend remembers saying. "He won't hurt you—he'll just run away. I've seen lots of them."

If I know the "name" of a computer, a space rocket or a mushroom, I know how to react. I know something of its nature and its function, and I know that some people, at least, can "control" it.

In the second story of creation in the Bible, God formed various wild animals and various birds out of the ground and "brought them to the man to see what he would call them; whatever the man called each of them would be its name" (Genesis 2:19). In the mindset of the biblical writers, this meant that Adam had control over creation, given him by God (Genesis 1:28).

What has all this to do with God? Let's start with Moses. When God appeared to him in the burning bush, Moses said, "What is your name?" And God wouldn't tell him.

The biblical writers had two reasons for this. First, they wanted to reject the magic of their pagan neighbors, who used the names of their gods in ritual incantations, supposedly acquiring power thereby.

Second, they wanted to show that no one can know the name of God because, to rephrase the Arab's reply above, God's name *is* God, and no one can "know" God in the sense of fully comprehending who or what God is. So God gave Moses a mysterious answer: "Yahweh" ("I am who I am" or "I am who am"), meaning that God is the uncaused source of all being. He just *is*; he is not caused. Being is his by nature, not by birth or creation.

So, to know the name of God is to know his essence, his inmost nature, his being. And that is impossible, except to God himself.

There is no human word or idea that can express who God is. God is not "another" being among those he creates. He is the ground of all being.

But the Jews did not think in these later (Greek,

philosophical) terms. Though the name "Yahweh" did not reveal the intimate nature of God, it did tell what God *does*: They sensed that "I am" meant "I will be present to you: I will be your protector, helper."

So holy was the name "Yahweh" that, in time, the Jews did not even pronounce it, partly out of awe for the formidable mystery, and partly because they feared that, if the pagans learned the name, they would use it in magical rites. So the Jews omitted the vowels of the word YAHWEH, and the resulting YHWH became the sacred "tetragrammaton"—literally, "four letters."

What does all this mean, practically? It means that we really don't *have* the name of God; that is, we don't have his nature, his being, his essence under the control of our understanding. But on the other hand, Jesus did give us his own "name" for God: "*Abba*, dear Father," the gentle one with whom I can have the greatest intimacy and childlike familiarity.

One balances the other. I can be a trusting little child whom God holds in his arms, and I am still the totally dependent creature who must bow down in adoration before the unspeakably Holy One. I cannot make God a pal, but I can't put him in unreachable space, either.

So, hallowed be God.

How?

'You Alone Are Holy'

We have already seen that "Abba" is a child's intimate expression of trust, love and peace. But the name of God also invokes the greatest "distance" and corresponding awe.

Now, if the name of God—that is, God—is mystery, and utterly beyond our comprehension, how can we hallow "it" or hallow God?

To hallow is to make holy. We can (we think) do this in three ways: 1) We can make something holy that was not, in our opinion, holy before; for instance, we can consecrate a precious goblet and use it only at the Eucharist. 2) We can treat someone or something with reverence, awe; never lightly or disrespectfully. 3) We can use the word as Scripture does, to mean that God is totally, absolutely "other," "different" from all creatures. "My ways are not your ways." God is, again, not just one more being among many.

When this biblical idea of holiness is applied to everyday life, we have a problem. "Holy" means separated, different, removed from the ordinary. And this implies that everyday life really isn't worth much. You're not really "holy" unless you're separated from the run of humankind by becoming a Trappist, a Carmelite monk, a Poor Clare nun. And things like wood, water, food—even our bodies—are not holy unless they are blessed. This notion once led to a terrible chasm between some normally unreachable life and the "secular" of everyday life. Most people, as a result, can't think of themselves as holy. That's for special people, they say.

Vatican II reminded us that there is *only one holiness*, and that is God's. And *all* members of the Church are called to share this one holiness. It is not earned, it is received.

To return to God: Holiness is the very nature of God, and obviously only God can "hallow" his "name." Only God can "produce" this holiness.

Therefore when we speak about some "hallowing" to be done, it obviously refers to something God does *in us*. What we are saying is:

Father,
make your name holy in our minds and hearts.
Bring it about
that you are given that special perfect reverence and love
which only you deserve.
Help us realize a bit, in our finite minds, who you are.
Help us bow down in awe
as well as fascination before you.
You indeed dwell in inapproachable light—
but let that mysterious light shine in our hearts.

> *Let the whole world see your light,*
> *and respond to you with joy.*
> *Please do it!*

We don't hallow God's name; we pray that *God* will do it. The only thing we can do is get out of the way, not block the light or impede the flow of power. When Jesus said, "Let your light shine before men," he obviously meant a light *given* us, for he added immediately, "so that they may see your good works and glorify your Father who is in heaven." We are like light bulbs. We cannot produce God's light; we can only receive it. It is God who illumines—without our being able to "see" the cause.

When we ask God to hallow his name, we are asking that his holiness—his very being—be revealed: that is, that he may help us see that he is holiness or, simply, that he is God.

God's holiness was revealed in the most perfect way—so far in history—by Jesus. But in Jesus that holiness was veiled by humanity. It takes faith to "see" the holiness of God in Jesus.

I just said "so far." As we shall see, most scholars see Matthew's version of the Our Father as an *"end-time"* prayer—that is, a prayer that pleads for God to make the final intervention and bring to a glorious conclusion all his plans through history; in other words, the end of the world. In that sense what we are praying is, "Make your holiness evident *now, once and for all.* Open wide your glory. Make the final manifestation." In this spirit the early Church prayed, "Come, Lord Jesus."

And Peter Said, 'Lord, What About Us?'

Have you noticed that this petition has nothing to do with *our* holiness? It's all about God's. As Raissa Maritain has said, "He who would offer a worthy prayer to God should ask for nothing but the Father's glory, but should make everything else come after the praise of him." This cleanses us of egotism, for all that we do is meaningless unless it is done to glorify God—that is, to let his holiness shine through our lives.

We have a problem, or a paradox, here. Leon-Dufour says that holiness is "a complex reality which touches on the mystery of God." Therefore, holiness seems to be "inaccessibly reserved for God, but is constantly attributed to creatures."

It's a case of ordinary people being wiser than the theologians. People do shy away from being called holy (even though Paul wrote to ordinary people in Corinth and called them "saints"). They are half right, because they sense that only God is holy. They are half wrong in thinking that holiness is an achievement of relatively few human beings, themselves not included. Holiness is not an achievement, it is a gift. We simply get out of the way and let God's love—and the power to love—possess our minds and hearts and bodies. We can, unbelievably, love like God.

'We Glorify You'

Another key word to be added to *name* and *hallowed* for understanding this prayer is *glory*.

Glory simply (though nothing is simple here, except that it is as simple as God) means the revealing of God's inaccessible holiness. It is seeing, with Moses, "the back of God as he passes." God's glory is his holiness shining forth to the eyes of loving faith.

Jesus is as much as we have seen of the glory of God. In his prayer to the Father at the Last Supper, he said, "I have given you glory....I have let your infinite holiness shine through me....Now glorify your son....Let people see who I am: not just this human being, but your eternal Son" (cf. John 17:4, 6, 25-26).

We hallow God's name by "giving" him glory. We have nothing to give; but our Brother, Jesus, prays with us in the life of the Church, and the Spirit of God "sighs within us with unspeakable groaning." We hallow God's name by letting his holiness be seen in our lives—when people really realize that there's something more here than mere human achievement.

God has put his name—himself—into our hands, to hallow or profane. Only God can make his name holy, but he can do it only through those who let their eyes be opened to perceive glory.

Glory is given most perfectly in the communion of human beings. "Where two or three are gathered in my name, I am there in the midst of them"—which means that because Jesus is present, God and man, God is perfectly honored, his name is duly hallowed.

The purpose of the Church, as Evelyn Underhill has noted, is the more perfect hallowing of the Name, "for the Church is the Body in and through which the Son, the Logos, utters the praises of the Father. Men are redeemed out of slavery to time into the freedom of eternal life, that they may take their small part in this eternal act of sacrificial worship." All Christian life begins and ends in acknowledging and praising the name of God in word and action.

'We Adore Thee'

Still another key word needs to be added to the other three: *adoration*. Again quoting Evelyn Underhill, adoration is "a delighted recognition of the life and action of God, subordinating everything to the presence of the Holy. It is the essential preparation for action. It stops all feverish strain, all rebellion and despondency about our own importance, all worry about our own success."

The more we glorify God and, as it were, forget about ourselves, the more we benefit. If we die, we live. If we "let loose" of life, we get life. To hallow God's name means to *let God alone be Lord*. It means surrendering life into his hands. This is the way the Father draws us to himself. "No one can come to me, unless the Father draw him." We can't become new persons by deciding to become new persons. God makes us new. Through those who are born again through the Holy Spirit, God hallows his name. He alone lets his glory shine through them.

What we are praying for in this second petition was well said by Zechariah: "The LORD shall become king over all the earth; on that day the LORD shall be the only one, and his name the only one" (14:9).

The ultimate purpose of life is not primarily the sanctification of the world, but the "making holy" of God. Holiness is not a turning in on ourselves, but a lifting of our eyes to see and receive the glory of God.

God,
Yahweh,
Eternal One,
We dare to speak to you,
because you have given us your true name—
Abba.
Our lips have spoken many foolish words,
cruel and selfish words.
Cleanse them now,
so that the holiness of your name
may flow out to the world from each of us, your children.
You alone are the Holy One,
you alone are goodness and love, being and eternity.
Let your holiness blaze out over the world in the hearts of
*   all creatures.*
Forgive us the pride that clings to our self-made virtue,
and the arrogance with which we ignore you.
Let your power loose upon the world
to destroy all evil.
But let your love go with it,
for you are Abba,
whose name is mercy.

We pray for your glory.
May it break through the heavens,
so that all the world may see you.
We bow down before that blinding beauty,

*and we know again that we are your needful creatures.
But we are more than that:
We are the children you love
with a love that is barely reflected in all the mothers and
 fathers of the world.
We dare to run to you, then, as your children,
to rest in your holiness.*

Matthew 6:10	*Luke 11:2*
your kingdom come, (NAB, JB)	Same
Thy kingdom come, (RSV)	Same

III

'Thy Kingdom Come'

There's been a lot of kingly and queenly withering in recent centuries, and the words "king" and "kingdom" need a lot of transforming from a very diluted and often disgraceful condition before we can pray "Thy kingdom come" with the full enthusiasm Jesus wants.

On the face of it, Jesus doesn't seem to have helped much in defining just what the "Kingdom" is. You won't find a verse in the New Testament that says, "The Kingdom of God means *precisely* this." He just said that the Kingdom is *something like* this.

Obviously it has something to do with God, and there are people involved. It's not a place on the globe, and it's not even the whole world. We don't know who on earth belongs. Members of the Church belong—except those who don't; and we don't know for sure who *those* are. But the Church is not the Kingdom: There are Kingdom people "out there" too. The Kingdom is now, but it's going to come someday in the future. Jesus is King of kings, but someday he'll "hand over" the Kingdom to the Father, and God will be all in all.

Meantime, what are we praying for?

Somewhere along the line we'll come up with a definition arrived at by wise theologians. But we must be careful not to think they have captured the full meaning—if for no other reason than that God is involved, and God is, finally, mystery.

Jesus didn't give a definition, but he does offer us 29 stories and comparisons which tell us what the Kingdom is *like*. His expression is, "The reign of God *may be likened* [for instance] to a man who sowed good seed in his field" (Matthew 13:24). These are, of course, the "parables of the Kingdom" which are so prominent in the first three Gospels.

We can do no better than to start with them. What do they say the Kingdom is "like"?

First, the Kingdom is free. It is God's gift, and nobody earns it. God goes out into the highways and byways of the world and invites anybody and everybody to the banquet (see Matthew 22:9).

The Kingdom doesn't run on its members' brains, talent, power or holiness. It has power built into it. It's not a huge battery God created, or even a "soul." It is God himself, making the Kingdom grow from within—the way yeast works through a mass of dough, or a seed the size of a dot becomes a tree where birds make their nests (see Matthew 13:32, 33). The power is unstoppable, so the members don't have to worry about the Kingdom's continuing—only their membership. It grows of itself: The farmer puts seed in the ground and goes about his business—and the seed grows of itself, producing blade, ear and ripe wheat (see Mark 4:26).

Since the world has messed itself up so much, the Kingdom has very few totally innocent members. Some members are smart-aleck kids who run off to the big city while their Father waits patiently at the door to embrace them when they come back (see Luke 15:11-24). Jesus took the sinning for granted; what he kept exulting about was the joy of the Father on their return (see Luke 15:7).

As it appears to the eyes of the world, in its present state, the Kingdom looks like a lot of Harrys and Helens rounded up off the streets. Some are weeds, some real wheat (see Matthew 13:24-30). (Some look like weeds but aren't, and some look like wheat but aren't.) It's only after they've felt the power of the invitation that they can decide to stay and submit to being saved.

If you ever saw the mess on the deck of a shrimp boat on the Mississippi, after the shrimp have been dumped out of the net, you would know what Jesus meant when he said the Kingdom is like a dragnet which "collected all sorts of things" (Matthew 13:47). Strangely, in our view, God doesn't clean up the deck right away. And, in the other comparison, he lets the weeds grow for all they're worth.

But there will come a day of harvest, and a day when only what the shrimper wants will be separated out (see Matthew 13:30). The door that was open since Adam will be closed (see Luke 13:25). The tree that was allowed to stand unfruitful year after year will finally be cut down (see Luke 13:6-7). There will be an unbridgeable gap between the poor man now in Abraham's bosom and the rich man who made that kind of gap on earth (see Luke 16:19-31).

The Kingdom is a pearl (see Matthew 13:45). Empty all the banks in the world and buy it. It's a treasure, hidden beneath the ground where armies and revelers tread (see Matthew 13:44).

Still, you can't buy your way in. It's only for people who know that the gift they properly receive is mercy, not wages (see Matthew 20:1-16). It's for people who don't strut before the altar bearing their gifts, but stand in the back like beggars—thin beggars, heart-quickened, but still beggars (see Luke 18:9-14).

Everything's free in the Kingdom—admission, board and room. Not all the merit in the world can buy a reservation. But once in, the residents have to act like the King. When they find someone like themselves lying in the gutter, they have to postpone their lectures on charity and pick up the ragged one and carry him inside (see Luke 10:25-37). If they don't, the King will discover that they themselves are still wearing earthly finery, instead of the rags of the Kingdom. The name of the Kingdom is endless mercy (see Matthew 22:1-14).

In spite of all this, there are some who can't let God have his Kingdom. They steal God's land and form their own. They kill the agents God sends to claim ownership—even the owner's Son (see Mark 12:1-9).

The books of the Kingdom are always unbalanced. The coin is mercy received and mercy given. But woe to those who don't match the King's millions with a dollar of their own. They will find themselves penniless outside the gate (see Matthew 18:23-34).

A strange thing about the Kingdom: The members at the banquet table are like children of the house—yet they must constantly beg to enter, as if they were still outside. They must knock insistently on the door they have already entered. They must call until the King comes and embraces them (see Luke 11:5-8).

The Kingdom is here already, of course, and of course it's still coming (see Matthew 12:28; Mark 9:1). After we have it, the King makes a great point of the need to watch for its coming (see Matthew 24:43-51). We must be able, like the old Indians, to "read sign" where others see only sand. The King comes like a mother to pick up a crying baby at night, but we must watch for him like sentinels whose eyes constantly sweep the darkness, or like detectives stalking a criminal. Those who think the bus is going to wait for them will later phone in vain. "No such name on the guest list" (see Matthew 25:12).

The Kingdom is only for wise people, those who sit down and make very practical decisions, such as, "We don't have enough money to buy tickets, so let's go where they're giving them away free."

The Kingdom is here, and the Kingdom will come, on the great Day of the Lord when they read the will. Those who think they have rights to the family fortune are going to be disappointed, for the lawyer will lift his eyebrows and announce that all the money goes to those people across the road who shared their trailer with stranded motorists, runaways and Okies on their way west.

The reason for this, the will reads, is that "I wanted to see if they would take me in if I was worse off than they were—and they did" (see Matthew 25:31-40).

Can you find a definition of the Kingdom somewhere in these wonderful parables of Jesus? Maybe we're with St. Augustine when he was asked to define "time." "If you don't ask me, I know what it is," he said. "But if you ask me, I don't know."

We're praying that *God* do something—which, of course, he is already doing. He is bringing the Kingdom into being. It is coming—or coming along, as we say. But we are also asking that God make it come once and for all, so that his glorious plan is finally, fully completed—all that he wished from eternity (another way of asking that his will be done, and his name be hallowed).

We surely can't make the Kingdom come, and yet there wouldn't be any Kingdom if God hadn't made us. So, in a sense, the Kingdom comes if we allow God to give us faith and hope and love and thus form the Kingdom.

It is a delicate matter. God does not press us, yet he plants the seed of desire for him in our hearts.

The Kingdom is like the gentle breeze Elijah experienced. Yet, seen as the power of God sweeping over the earth, it comes with "violence." It is a flood of energy that transforms, not destroys. It is the very life of God that irresistibly carries its beloved ones to eternal life. And yet, free human beings can withstand it like granite mountains.

The Kingdom and Jesus

From creation on the Kingdom has been growing. It became visible in Jesus, the eternal Son. He is the fullest flowering of what it means to be a member, even though he is the King. He revealed it gradually, in parables. He unleashed its power, again gradually, with "signs" of its presence—destroying the power of sin and all evil, sickness, suffering.

The Kingdom came in power with Jesus' death and resurrection, when he won the Kingdom by being defeated by evil. The Kingdom came to perfect fruition in his heart when he gathered up his whole life and love—and the whole human race—and said, "Father, into your hands I commend my spirit," and leaped into the darkness of death in perfect trust.

And the Father lifted him up from death, up to eternal life, up to exaltation "at his right hand" with the glory "I had, Father, from all eternity." Now he is made "Son of God in power," able to unite all human flesh and spirit to himself, never again to be separated from God.

The Kingdom rushed out into the world with the flame of Pentecost, nourished by the death and resurrection of its Lord, and constantly growing by the power of the Spirit.

It is a mysterious reality, known only by the poor in spirit, not the worldly-wise and prudent.

The Church is the Kingdom of God "in mystery"; that is, it is a sign and sacrament of the Kingdom just as it is a sign of Jesus. But the Church is not the Kingdom. It is the initial budding of the Kingdom. The Coming of Jesus will mean the end of the Church. Then Jesus will hand over "his" Kingdom to the Father.

The Kingdom now is God possessing all who open themselves to his self-revealing and self-giving. The final Kingdom will be the same. The difference is that at the present time the door is still open.

The final Kingdom will be the fulfilling of all the desires of God's people—the fulfilling of God's own eternal desire and plan. Then God will be seen as the Lord of history, and all those who have lovingly subjected themselves to him will see his glory.

We pray that the Kingdom be fulfilled today, every day; and we pray that it be fulfilled once and for all. In Matthew, the emphasis is on the "once and for all." A perfect prayer would want the latter—God's total and perfect glorification—the end, the fulfillment, the destruction of all evil, the perfect adoration of God by his people. Now, once and for all.

But, of course, if God wants to do it in stages, God's will be done. The saint wants the Kingdom to come now, once and for all, because then God will be more perfectly honored, totally visible, unspoiledly loved. The saintly man or woman who wants all that God has wanted from eternity—and wants it perfectly fulfilled—is, in a sense, impatient, yet perfectly attuned to the patience of God.

Sinners that we are, we tend to paint the Day of the Lord in dark tones of tragedy. Tragedy it will be, for some. That is the mystery of evil and of the perversion of freedom. When we pray the Our Father we are joining God's saving love as he tries to save people from the inbreeding of their freedom, from an eternally foolish choice. Implicitly, the prayer says to the world, "Repent and believe the Good News!"

But it will be the Greatest Day, our final liberation into the peace of God. Then vision will widen and deepen beyond all horizons and we will have what we were made for.

Abba,
may your Kingdom come.
You establish your loving rule in our hearts
without our deserving it.
We thank you.
You alone can make your Kingdom grow.
Even our response is your gift.
Even when we run away from your will,
your welcome never changes.
We have nothing to contribute,
except your gifts.
We are unprofitable servants,
but you make us your truly begotten children.
When you rule our minds and hearts,
it is worth more than all the power and pleasure and treasure
   in the world.
Help us never to deceive ourselves,
but to see you always with clear eyes
and love you with pure hearts.
May the full glory of your love fill the whole world!

Matthew 6:10	Not in Luke*

your will be done
on earth as it is in heaven.
(NAB)

your will be done,
on earth as in heaven. (JB)

Thy will be done
   On earth as it is in
   heaven. (RSV)

---

*It is remarkable that this petition does not appear in Luke's version of the Our Father. It seems fair to say that Matthew certainly didn't just add it. Nor would Luke have chosen to omit it. It would seem that the Church in the north of Palestine preserved a saying of Jesus which was somehow not remembered by the Christians for whom Luke wrote. The petition reflects Matthew's emphasis—greater than Mark's or Luke's—on doing God's will as a central element of Christian holiness.

IV

'THY WILL BE DONE ON EARTH AS IT IS IN HEAVEN'

A chemical plant explodes in India, and 2,500 people die. Is this "God's will"?

Archbishop Romero stands at an altar in El Salvador. He has dared to denounce death squads, oppression of the poor. A bullet stops his voice forever. Is this "God's will"?

A man and a woman exchange golden rings and lock themselves in each other's arms. Is this "God's will"?

Two tots run in circles in the grass, shrieking with delight, arms swooping like airplane wings.

The sun rises....

God is patient, or, as the old catechisms used to say, long-suffering. He allows us to abuse and distort and falsify a phrase which should be used to describe all that is loving and lovely about God: *God's will*. Crusades, not always as Christian as they professed to be, rode on the enthusiasm produced by the phrase. Crimes were committed in its name. Authority in religious life used it to obtain blind obedience. And the suffering of all ages have looked in the face of heaven and seen something cold and unfair in that stark phrase.

It is as if we believed in the good and loving God on the one hand, and then extracted something called "God's will" on the other. The two didn't fit together, but it was

"God's will" that we accept the apparent contradiction. "God's will" sometimes seems to express something unreasonable about God. So, if we are to experience the riches of this prayer, we must first deal with the most "unreasonable" thing in our lives: suffering and death.

When suffering is actually upon us—the grip of bodily pain, the sword of contradiction, cold despair—we grasp at straws of "explanation." Finding none, we grit our teeth and bow before a distant, impersonal God (who is, after all, our only hope, even if a heartless friend), or we slip the bonds of fear and shake our fists in the face of heaven.

Even the "holy" can fall into a certain self-satisfied "resignation" when they say, "Your will be done." God is unreasonable, but he has to be humored, like an aged uncle. He has not been totally generous with us, but we have borne up bravely. We fit ourselves with martyrs' halos.

Beginning With Jesus

Of all the ways of approaching the problem, the most obvious for Christians is to begin with Jesus, indeed the Jesus of Gethsemane. "My Father, if it is possible, let this cup pass me by. Still, let it be as you would have it, not as I" (Matthew 26:39).

Was he quarreling with his Father? Was he really trying to make his Father change his mind?

Well, can you imagine such a prayer being *heard*? Can you imagine the Father releasing him from his eternal vocation, so that he could walk unharmed through the ranks of the temple police and go—where? To pleasant retirement on the banks of the Nile? To a "teaching job" in Rome? Or to a quiet disappearance—a failed Messiah?

John's Gospel has Jesus explicitly rejecting this possibility a week before his death:

> "My soul is troubled now,
> yet what should I say—
> Father, save me from this hour?
> But it was for this that I came to this hour.
> Father, glorify your name!" (John 12:27-28)

What *must* Jesus have meant when he prayed, "If it is possible..."? First, he prayed as a human being who had tasted the wonder of human life more deeply than anyone in history. His whole being could do nothing but shrink in horror from the prospect of having this precious life destroyed. No one had ever embraced life so eagerly. His sensitive heart and mind, unspoiled and childlike, saw the full malice of death, sin, hatred, betrayal, the arrogant injustice of the evil closing in on him. He hated all of it, with the full flaming energy of his will. As humanly as anyone ever looked about for a way out, he searched for escape. Naturally, humanly, there could be no other *primary* response but terror and revulsion.

Nevertheless he said, "Let it be as you would have it"—not according to this understandable but earthbound impulse of mine. Something deeper than horror filled his spirit—the total and absolute love and trust of his Father. It had been and still was the very food that kept him alive (John 4:34). His Father's love was the full, passionate joy that had come to possess him, down deep, a joy that rested on the vision and full tasting of his Father's love.

This was the *dominant* surge of conviction that welled up in him, even as he pressed his forehead into the earth in Gethsemane. He could do nothing about the horror that forced blood through his pores. It was there, like gravity, or darkness.

But if this was reality—and he did not foolishly deny it—there was a mightier reality that he welcomed with a powerful freedom. It rose above his human fear and reaffirmed his lifelong and total dedication.

The Mysterious 'Must' of Jesus' Death

One aspect of Jesus' suffering and death must not be overlooked: According to the Gospels, especially Luke, Jesus *had* to die:

"The Son of Man *must*...be put to death, and then be raised up on the third day." (9:22)

"I *must* proceed on course today, tomorrow and the day after, since no prophet can be allowed to die anywhere except in Jerusalem." (13:33)

"First, however, he *must* suffer much." (17:25)

"'He was counted among the wicked,' and this, I tell you, *must* come to be fulfilled in me." (22:37)

"Remember what he said to you while he was still in Galilee—that the Son of Man *must* be delivered into the hands of sinful men, and be crucified, and on the third day rise again." (24:6-7)

"Did not the Messiah *have to* undergo all this so as to enter into his glory?" (24:26)

In Acts, Luke has several references to the same "must" in the lives of Jesus' followers.

What "must" this mean? Certainly it is not the sadistic order of a God who could be pleased or "satisfied" with torture. That would be a blasphemous concept. Nor could it be the unfeeling command of a sternly just Father which a dutiful son would grimly obey.

Rather, to use human terms about an unfathomable mystery, it was something "worked out" in the heart of the Trinity. The Son would become a creature who would stand in the midst of his brothers and sisters and offer the greatest symbol of a creature's obedience and love—the giving back of life to the Giver. He would *choose* to die with full freedom, with a child's simple, gentle trust.

The "must" was that he had to go the whole way. There is nothing greater that anyone can give than life. It would not have been enough to *profess* this willingness, or even to show it in a thousand loving ways short of death. He had to *do* it. He had to choose to throw himself down into the darkness of death, knowing that his Father's arms were there to bear him up as soon as he passed through the veil—yet needing to trust that this would happen, just as any other human being must trust the Father who cannot be seen or heard.

Jesus knew his vocation. Gradually it became clear to him that it must all end in his death. He *must* show the world the supreme example of a creature's proper response to God: total and absolute submission, obedience and dependence, all resting in childlike gratitude, trust and joy.

Joy was not *defeated*. We don't need to say that his Father's will "overcame" Jesus. Rather, "Your will be done" was Jesus' final, perfect maturing to freedom—a freedom that could be fully exercised in spite of the most painful counterattack of human reluctance.

So he walked boldly from Gethsemane to face the might of the world—swords, clubs, the *man*power of his enemies.

The Father's raising Jesus from the dead was the inevitable result of his freely dying. This pure human being could not possibly be separated from his Father, or from that full inheritance the Father had planned for all his children.

Jesus thus saved us by his death/resurrection, his perfect obedience and love. But not automatically, like someone who pays for our release from prison even though our attitude does not change. "Your attitude must be that of Christ" (Philippians 2:5).

Our 'Must'

A "must" exists for us too. We must show the total dependence and childlikeness that Jesus had. We must die many times before our death by daily surrenderings of selfishness—always being raised to greater life—until the day when we willingly surrender our very life as he did.

In Jesus, human nature is reunited to God, inseparably, forever. Anyone, therefore, who is united to Jesus is reunited to the Father, *saved*. Obviously this union must be free, deliberate, personal. We are not going to heaven in a sugar bowl because someone named Jesus died back there somewhere. We are going to heaven if we go the way he did. He is, literally, the way. Taking up our cross doesn't mean looking around for painful situations to bear. It means the same willingness to die that Jesus had—the choice of giving up absolutely everything as a sign and symbol of total obedience, trust and love of the Father.

Jesus said, for every human being (and every human being is called to do the same),

*You are my God,
and all I have is yours.
You love me with the Father's tenderest love,
and I am as totally dependent on you
as a newborn baby in its mother's arms.
I have no independence of my own.
I owe you everything.
And I must be totally convinced of this and express it.*

And we must add what Jesus could not say, for he could speak as a human being but not as a sinful one:

*We have dared to stand before you and assert our
 independence.
We have claimed equality with you—
the right to do as we please with our life,
as if we had created it.
We have refused to be creatures—
totally in your debt, needing to receive everything from you.
And this pitiful, ridiculous posturing must be rejected.
We must return to you,*

*a loving Father but also one on whom we are totally
   dependent.
We must return, not like slaves,
but still as totally repentant children who possess nothing
   by right.
We must come to our senses
and let you purify our hearts and minds.
You offer happiness;
we chose "reasonable" rebellion.
You are the infinite,
the mysterious,
the awe-full,
and yet the tender,
the merciful,
the gentle.
We beg the grace of sorrow, penance, mercy.
We have no hope apart from you.
There is no escape from our misery except in your grace.
And you do give your grace, your Self.*

    We join Jesus in his total trust, and we add our sorrow for sin.

God's Will Is Our Freedom

The priceless value of Jesus' death lies in his freedom. At the heart of all "explanations" of God's will and suffering is the priceless gift of *our* freedom.

    The fundamental fact is that God gave us freedom and he *never takes it back*. Others may take it *away*, with drugs or torture, but God puts no limits on our ability to choose. That is the amazing mystery of freedom. We can destroy God's world, kill his Son and reject his love. And God waits.

    Putting it all in distorted human terms, we can imagine God trying to decide whether to give freedom to these marvelous beings he was going to create. The odds were against success. Whether God contemplated a few hundred people or the four billion on the earth today, it was almost certain that some of them would abuse this gift of freedom and use it to choose evil.

This meant they would not only hurt themselves, but that others— innocent, holy people—would be hurt, killed, libeled, insulted, demeaned.

God might have decided against the whole idea. He might have created a world of machinery, perfectly oiled, whirring in dull and monotonous perfection. A robot could be programmed never to shoot another robot, and certainly a word processor would never libel a mimeograph machine. A computer would never think of committing adultery.

Perfect. And eternally dull.

So God opted for freedom, and the cost of that decision was all the pain and cruelty and suffering in life. He had to permit all this if he was going to have free children who would love him with a force that nothing could withstand. If we can imagine God being thrilled with the prospect of what he had done, we can think of him as seeing all the Francises and Teresas loving the "unlovable"; all the husbands and wives giving faithful love to each other and their children; all the mothers tenderly caring for retarded children; all the heroes dying that others might live; all the gentle lads giving up their lunch money to buy a gift for their mothers; all the teachers patiently leading troubled children; all the fathers hurrying home.

Theoretically this sounds good—especially if you're not suffering anything at the moment. But the discussion doesn't really get going until someone says, "But couldn't God stop *some* of the evil?"

Pursue that idea. If God decides to deflect the bullet that ends John Kennedy's life, why not the one that kills a poor black in South Africa? Then, why not *all* bullets, all knives, bombs, fists, clubs, arrows?

If God is to spare your family the pain of sickness (whether from natural causes or from human folly), why not the family across the street? Why not everybody on your street, everybody in the world?

If God is to spare a wife the pain of her husband's infidelity—and how else could God do this except by miraculously erasing all temptation from mind and body—why not excise the lust in all would-be adulterers, rapists, porn merchants?

There is only one logical conclusion to all this: God would have to stop all freedom. Everything would be forced. No evil could happen.

If I were forced to love and forgive my neighbor, it would not be love, but a response like that of one chemical reacting to another. If there can be no sinners, there can be no saints. If there can be no hate, there can be no love. If there are to be heroes and heroines, even garden-variety ones as on your street, there must also be cowards, liars and thieves.

God must accept partial defeat for the sake of final victory. He must permit sin in the sense of not destroying the freedom of the sinner—just as a parent permits the insolence of a child by not taping its mouth shut. Why? Because all the freely given love in the world will last forever; it has the eternal divine within it and will never cease being beautiful.

Theoretically, again, this argument is irrefutable. But it would be totally useless and even terribly unfeeling for anyone to try it with a mother whose children have just died in a fire, or a father whose son has hanged himself, or a child who knows that her parents will never come home again.

Sometimes the only solace is to pray with Jesus the psalm he prayed on the cross: "My God, my God, why have you forsaken me?"—and to go *all the way through the psalm to the end*. In the course of the psalm the *same speaker* says,

> I will proclaim your name to my brethren;
>   in the midst of the assembly I will praise you:
> "You who fear the LORD, praise him....
> For he has not spurned nor disdained
>   the wretched man in his misery,

>Nor did he turn his face away from him,
>>but when he cried out to him, he heard him."
>So by your gift will I utter praise in the vast
>>assembly....
>The lowly shall eat their fill;
>>they who seek the LORD shall praise him:
>"May your hearts be ever merry!"
>>(Psalm 22:23-24a, 25-26a, 27)

What does this "explanation" do to prayer? Isn't it useless to pray, since God must permit free will?

So Why Pray?

There is no simple answer to this, either. There have been thousands and thousands of people, saints included, who have prayed that war be averted, that cruelty be stopped, that wayward sons and daughters return, that sickness be cured, that justice be done. The list has no end.

Obviously, they didn't always get what they asked for. Perhaps seldom. To imagine God granting everything anyone asks for is to find the same deadlock as when one imagines God stopping every evil. But Jesus said, "Whatever you ask in my name I will give you." What can this mean?

"In my name" includes the whole mystery of the gospel, Jesus' death and resurrection, Jesus' very spirit. It is the spirit that fills those who pray together, who pray for each other, who join hands to let the power of God flow in and out of them, who pray as Jesus did on the cross—but also at the Last Supper.

People who pray "in Jesus' name" still suffer, they still weep and they still die. But a Christlike thing happens among them, inside them—peace, trust, godlikeness. God saw that, from eternity, and decided that freedom was worth the price.

The results are not far to seek. I have a friend who spends a large part of each Thursday visiting patients in a hospital. One day she met a man who had returned for treatment—a "repeater." He had been diagnosed as hydrocephalic and consequently suffered terrible headaches. A shunt had been placed in his head to drain the fluid, after which his doctor literally hung out his sign—"left town"—and took his patient's files with him.

The shunt was now clogged and he was back in the hospital. He and his wife, my friend relates, were simple, hardworking people, "so faith-filled that it gives me goose bumps."

One day as my friend prayed the Our Father with this man, he suddenly stopped after the words "Thy will be done" and said, "That's it! That's where it is! His will is that I live each day for him through all of this and never let go of the happiness he gives me." He smiled and continued, "on earth as it is in heaven."

Well, Then, How Should We Pray?

I hope all that has been said about suffering and God's will is helpful. It seems necessary, even if it sounds theoretical, cold-blooded and severe. But now, supposing we have a trusting, patient attitude, what is the *positive* thrust of our prayer?

First, as in the "hallowed" petition, we are praying that *God* do something. We are not primarily praying for our own virtue, except, of course, insofar as it is implied as a consequence of God's creating grace. But the very phrasing of this request is an example of Jewish/biblical reverence for God's name. "Hallowed *be* thy name" and "Thy will *be* done" are reverent ways of saying, "God, hallow your name!" and "God, do your will!"

This is not just a matter of style. Only God can do God's will. Only by the grace of God—that is, God somehow doing it in us—can we do anything.

Paul says, "God is at work in you, both to will and to work for his good pleasure" (Philippians 2:13). And there is always that striking statement in one of the Mass

Prefaces: "Even our desire to please you is your gift."

What must God do, then, in exercising his will? He must, as Jesus said, "draw all things to himself" now that Jesus has been "lifted up." We must again recall Jesus' words, "No one can come to me, unless the Father draw him," and his admonition to Simon Peter: "Flesh and blood have not revealed this to you [that is, that Jesus is the Messiah] but my Father who is in heaven" (Matthew 16:17).

Originally, God's will was that all creatures recognize him as the source of all life and love, happiness and peace, and offer their lives to him in trustful response. But this plan was obstructed by sin. Then God's will became the saving of every human being from the slavery and misery of sin into which the whole world was plunged. God "wants all men to be saved and come to know the truth" (1 Timothy 2:4). Indeed, Paul reminds us, "...the world itself will be freed from its slavery to corruption and share in the glorious freedom of the children of God" (Romans 8:21); that is, *material creation* will share the glory of redeemed humanity.

When we pray, therefore, we are asking God to create in every human being on earth the childlike trust that was in Jesus. This should normally be done through his giving us a knowledge and love of Jesus, in a community. But even those who have never heard of Jesus, or who have seen only a distorted picture of Jesus, can experience God's grace in their hearts without being aware that it is the grace of Jesus. God gives such people the invitation to grace and the power to respond—always according to their ability, their culture. If they do "what in them lies" they are what Karl Rahner has called "anonymous Christians."

'Do Your Love!'

God is simple in a way we cannot understand. God has no parts. He is not split into mind, will, heart, being, etc. His being *is* his heart, his mind *is* his love. God *is* love, as John says.

When we pray, "Your will be done," we are praying,

God,
good Father,
do your loving!
Love as only you can love!
Be God!
*Be love!**

As in so many prayers that the Church says, notice that we are praying for what *we are absolutely certain God is already doing*. We are "merely" expressing our total dependence on that love.

God's 'Further' Will

God's will is that we be holy. Again, we are not primarily praying that *we* do something, but that God do what he is already doing: "Give us a share of your life."

God's holiness is twofold. First, it is his way of being. To be holy is to be God. To be God is to be holy. This is not mere moral goodness. To be holy—to be God—is to be totally Other. In this case, of course, we are asking for the impossible—Godness. We are saying, "Give us a share of your very being." Scripture teaches us to believe that this impossible *is* possible, when it says, "He [God] has bestowed on us the great and precious things he promised, so that through these you who have fled a world corrupted by lust might become *sharers of the divine nature*" (2 Peter 1:4; emphasis added).

---

* We must note again that Matthew's version of the Gospel is, in the opinion of reputable scholars, an end-time prayer. That is, it asked God to bring his plan to fulfillment *now, or soon*. The death and resurrection of Jesus was the perfect fulfillment of God's will and plan. But the primary purpose still remained to be achieved—the eternal, face-to-face union of God and his creatures, those who had accepted his grace. As an end-time prayer, Matthew's Our Father presumed that this total fulfillment would come soon, and prayed for this with a great sense of urgency.

We share God's nature by being "graced." Then we can know as God knows, love as God loves. What looks like ordinary human wisdom and love is divine in those who open themselves to God's invitation to friendship.

Second, God's holiness is to be loving. This refers primarily to the mystery of the Trinity "where" life is an eternal and infinite outpouring and receiving of love. This is the *good* God. In this second meaning, to be the holy God is to be the good and loving God.

All the above is primary, and should be our primary awareness, the one thing we must never forget. Growing out of this fundamental humility and trust, obviously, is a life of manifold virtue—single actions created by God's grace—the kindness, healing, forgiveness, trust, courage, generosity, etc., of Jesus.

Summing up, we pray:

God,
our Father,
we are totally dependent on you.
You are Creator,
you are love.
Never cease doing what you are doing.
Do your love.
Create love in us
so that in Jesus we can love and praise you forever,
face-to-face.
Create the trust of little children in us.
Create us as your children of nature and grace.
Be God!

Why 'On Earth as It Is in Heaven'?

How is God's will done "in heaven"?

Heaven is God, or being with God. We are asking that God create on earth the same life and love that exists in the Trinity—the Father giving himself to the Son, the Son giving himself totally to the Father, the Spirit being the very "sigh" of their love.

Heaven is also the union of angels and saints—all the created beings (including a lot of "ordinary" people you knew) in whom God's will is now perfectly fulfilled.*

It is fulfilled in them by what they are—loving beings created in the Spirit, forever united to God. In them God's will is done completely. They are flooded, possessed, filled with the divine being and love. Nothing can distract or deceive them.

Again, we are asking for what God is already "trying" to do—make us what he always wanted us to be. True, there are limitations of space and time which will be removed only by our death. We are asking that the limitations *we* put on God's giving be removed.

We are asking for the final and total destruction of all evil, sin, injustice, cruelty. In the end-time view of the prayer, we are asking that this be done now, soon.

We are asking for what we know will infallibly happen. We are praying for the fulfillment of the first Good News:

"Glory to God in high heaven!
Peace on earth to people of God's good will!"**

That's everybody.

---

* Let us recall a very simple doctrine which has been luridly misstated: To be with God is to be without the slightest impurity. If someone dies with this slightest impurity, somewhere "between" dying and seeing God face-to-face this impurity must be rejected, removed, forgiven. *We have no idea* (preachers and artists beware) of how this happens, where, etc. *If* it is necessary, it is simply the first heavenly gift of God. This, no more and no less, is the purification which has often been distorted in our descriptions of *purgatory*.

** The actual meaning of the angels' song heard by the shepherds was: "Glory to God in high heaven, peace on earth to those on whom his favor rests," which means, literally, "to people of *God's* good will," not, primarily, "people who have good will of their own."

Matthew 6:11	*Luke 11:3*
Give us today our daily bread, (NAB, JB) Give us this day our daily bread; (RSV)	Give us each day our daily bread. (NAB, JB, RSV)

V

'GIVE US THIS DAY OUR DAILY BREAD'

A worried father has begged Jesus to come and cure his daughter. On the way comes the bad news—don't bother, she's dead. He goes to the child's home anyway, and says to the mourners, "She is not dead, just asleep." He takes her parents, plus Peter, James and John, into the room where the child lies. It is all very still and solemn. He bends over, takes the child by the hand, and says, "Get up, child." She gets up immediately. The five other adults besides Jesus just stand there holding their breath, motionless. They wait for the drama of the moment to strike them. Will she fall back? Is this real?

Here's a guess about what Jesus said next: "Well, are you going to stand there all day? Give her something to eat!"

The eternal and awe-full power of God has entered the room, driven death out the door, created one of those wild surmises in the minds of five people—and then turned the full power of its concern to providing bread for a child.

It was not a matter of moving from the sublime to the ridiculous, but the continuing mystery of the Word made *flesh*. God loves our bodies, too.

So far in the Our Father we have been praying about the deepest desires of God, the glory of his presence and power, the holiness of his being, the absolute necessity that he be loved and honored—and now God brings his majesty to our dinner table!

'Bread'

The first lesson of the petition "Give us this day our daily bread" is that it is a simple petition for bread—mere bread, earthly bread, something for our bodies. There are deep implications, of course, but we must not fall into the "spiritualism" of thinking that *only* the "spiritual" meanings are valid. The Our Father is a rainbow of several colors—including that of the flesh, which we sometimes tend to think is a cumbersome prison we drag around until the day of our liberation.

We cannot—or, should we say, *must* not—think of Jesus as frowning on "trivial" prayers—for your aunt's rheumatism, that Mark will make the team, that it won't rain on the parish picnic, that St. Anthony will find your false teeth. God condescended—without being "condescending"—to take our human flesh and blood, thereby declaring the preciousness of what he had created.

Little people—and who dares be anything else before God?—can talk about little things to him. Someone has noted that this request for bread resembles that of a little child suddenly crying out, at a solemn affair honoring a distinguished guest like the papal Secretary of State, "Mama, can I have a sandwich?"

God wants our stomachs reasonably full. He's interested in our breathing and sleeping, our sexuality and blood pressure, our muscles and bones, hormones and hair. Not just "tolerantly" interested because he made them and is now "stuck" with them; but *gladly*, because God makes only good things.

Someone is always trying to make us over into angels, trying to make us embarrassed about bodily functions and pleasures, making us feel a bit guilty if we think wine is fine and good digestion is a blessing and bodies are beautiful, if we relish the crack of ball upon bat or (like B-types) just lie in the sun and watch the birds fly over

God made us body-spirits, spirit-bodies. He wedded his divine nature *forever* to our human nature, flesh and blood, mind and heart, in Jesus. So it's O.K. to ask for the earthly:

Give us bread.
Give us the earth you gave us.

God meant a piece of the earth for everyone to develop, rest on and enjoy. A scandalous part of the world is deprived of that dignity today, while the powerful spend the wealth of the earth preparing to blow it up. God certainly didn't intend Lazarus to lie at the rich man's iron gate with dogs licking his sores, while the owner ate steak and pie inside.

'Daily'

Jesus didn't say, "Give us a good harvest" or "Please send a week's supply of groceries." The word *daily* makes a profound difference in the prayer. It is a prayer, first of all, of the poor. We depend on God day after day the way the institutionalized poor depend on someone to bring them their food every day. We live one day at a time.

The word that both Matthew and Luke use for "daily" is a Greek word found nowhere else in the Bible or in Greek literature. The sense probably is "Give us the bread we need every day." Not a year's or a lifetime's supply; just what is necessary, what we cannot live without. Even if it means "bread for the morrow," as some scholars think, it is still the prayer for one day—tomorrow—a workman's night prayer to make it one more day.

What better symbol of our total dependence on God than bread, the staff of life? When we pray this prayer, we are not only aware that God is interested in our earthly bodies and their food, but we are saying that our *life* absolutely depends on God. It is the prayer of those who have found the pearl of great price. They know the eternal value of their life, the love God has for them—us—and we pray,

> Thank you, Father, for our life.
> It is your gift.
> Please keep giving it to us.
> We are your children,
> and we are sure of your love for us.
> We simply present our needs to you,
> knowing that you will take care of them in wisdom and love.
> Protect the life of our bodies,
> our minds,
> our hearts.
> Give us strength to heal sickness,
> bring back the failing spirits of our brothers and sisters,
> rescue them from slavery and dishonor.
>
> We are in your hands.
> If we die,
> we have your life.
> If we live in pain,
> you are with us.
> If we are in health,
> you can spread the Kingdom through us.
>
> We beg you for what you always give:
> Jesus,
> your Son, our brother,
> our nourishment and our life,
> our union with you.

Right after the words of the Our Father in the Gospel of Matthew come Jesus' words about not being concerned for tomorrow, about what we shall eat or drink or put on. If his Father takes care of the birds of the air and the lilies of the field, how much more will he take care of us!

Does this mean we shouldn't have insurance, or plan that extra room, or pray for that better-paying job? Does it mean, in fact, that we shouldn't pray for anything except what we absolutely need today?

Of course not. God doesn't just want us to be alive at some minimum level, but to be fully human—to have the dignity of a home, and the opportunity to develop humanly and grace-iously by work and play, study, prayer, the intercommunion of a stable society. God certainly did not intend life to be a grim hanging on to bare existence. He meant life to be enjoyed. Otherwise he would not have created pleasure.

So there's no problem at all, is there? None whatever, unless Lazarus is sitting there outside our gate, the dogs licking his sores. There's nothing wrong at all about having tickets to the symphony or the ball game or the beach at Bermuda, unless we walk past that pitiful man sitting near the car we get into.

As long as there are no breadlines, we can all enjoy steak. When the children in Ethiopia are fed, we can have another round of drinks. When people don't burrow into cardboard boxes for the night, and bag ladies don't freeze in doorways, we can have color TV and a good furnace and even an Oldsmobile, if that's what they drive in your neighborhood.

'Our'

Jesus, of course, was thinking about all this. So he didn't say, "Give *me* today *my* daily bread." The world is *our* breadbox, and everybody gets in the same line.

If we were a hundred people on an island, and six of us owned 60 percent of the island, and 30 percent of it was a lake, and the other 10 percent had to be divided among the other 94 people, it would be embarrassing (hopefully) for the rich six to say, "Give *us* today *our* daily bread," without including all the rest. But in our world of four or five billion people, we find it hard to think of ourselves as that "little island."

When we pray, we ought to think of ourselves as joining hands in a circle that goes all the way around the world—with Russians and Chinese, Salvadorans and

Spaniards, Zulus and Afrikaners, communists and lepers and capitalists, bankers' sons at Choate and children playing on gangways of boats in Hong Kong harbor. Then we would either stop saying the words of the prayer, or we would try to rearrange the distribution of goods on the island.

Only 'Day After Day' or 'Once and for All'?

As we said earlier, Matthew's Our Father seems to be an end-time prayer; that is, those who prayed it, at least in the beginning, felt that Jesus was to return rather soon. From that viewpoint, "today" can be taken literally, or at least translated "soon."

Luke is more prosaic. Here, as in his entire Gospel, he is expressing the community's dawning realization that Jesus may be long in coming. He uses different words. Instead of Matthew's "Give us *today* our daily bread," he writes, "Give us our daily bread *day after day*"—that is, one day after another. It is a prayer of trust:

*Please continue to do
what we are sure your love makes you do:
Nourish us endlessly.*

It is possible that in Luke's community or communities the tension over the Second Coming had passed. The "return" of Jesus, for an indefinite length of time, was seen in the coming of his Spirit.

But one can easily imagine that in another community, both in faith and in the pain of persecution, Christians could express their yearning for the final coming of the final Banquet *today, soon*.

From this viewpoint, then, Christians can, and did, ask for the "bread of the future," God's final intervention, today. It could have been the prayer of those to whom Jesus said, "Blessed are you who hunger; you shall be filled."

Scripture frequently uses the metaphor of the banquet in the Kingdom. For instance, Jesus said, "Many will come from the east and the west and will find a place at the banquet in the kingdom of God with Abraham, Isaac and Jacob, while the natural heirs will be driven out into the dark" (Matthew 8:11-12). Since the second half of the statement refers to an end-time judgment, so, it would seem, does the first. Finally, Jesus promised the apostles that "in my kingdom you will eat and drink at my table, and you will sit on thrones judging the twelve tribes of Israel" (Luke 22:30). Further evidence that this petition in Matthew continues his end-time consciousness is the fact that the Greek word used implies a single action: again, once and for all.

The Eucharistic Bread

But the Eternal Banquet does already exist. We meet again the double factor of the Christian life: "already" and "not yet." All that the Scripture says about the Banquet, the Bread of Life, can obviously be predicated of the Eucharist. The fact that the Our Father is part of the Communion Rite of the Mass is a further reminder that the Christian mind and heart cannot think of "bread" without wanting the Bread of Life.

As we said above, God is interested in our having just plain bread to put into our mouths. That is the primary thrust of this petition. But it was inevitable that Christians should see other, and valid, meanings. Jesus himself said, "I am the Bread of Life," and when this prayer was said at the Eucharist, it would have been impossible not to think of the Eucharistic Bread that the Father would give his children that day.

In fact, those who hold that Matthew's version is both directed to the end-time and closer to Jesus' original will also hold that the Messianic banquet was primary in Jesus' mind.

Those who come to receive this bread hold out their

hands like those little children we see on television. There are few more striking symbols of utter dependence, childlikeness, hope, trust. We are totally dependent on Jesus, our Food; we are totally dependent on the bread that the Father puts on our kitchen table at home.

Both help us to strive for Jesus' ideal: "My food is to do the will of him who sent me."

Matthew 6:12	Luke 11:4
and forgive us the wrong we have done as we forgive those who wrong us. (NAB)	Forgive us our sins for we too forgive all who do us wrong; (NAB)
And forgive us our debts, As we have forgiven those who are in debt to us. (JB)	and forgive us our sins, for we ourselves forgive each one who is in debt to us. (JB)
And forgive us our debts, As we also have forgiven our debtors; (RSV)	and forgive us our sins, for we ourselves forgive everyone who is indebted to us; (RSV)

VI

'AND FORGIVE US OUR TRESPASSES AS WE FORGIVE THOSE WHO TRESPASS AGAINST US'

Once upon a time a strange thing happened at the 10:30 Mass at St. Michael's. Everything was going along smoothly and happily: pleasant, even stirring, music; the Penitential Rite easily disposed of; the Scripture readings professionally dramatized. There was a silence as the homilist had difficulty adjusting the microphone, but the people were settling in their pews, closing their eyes, and did not mind.

Then it came—a voice not human, but understandable; clear, unearthly, neither male nor female: "If you are bringing your gift to the altar, and there remember that your brother has something against you, leave your gift at the altar and go to be reconciled with your brother. Then come and offer your gift."

For the briefest second many thought it was a gimmick, or a freak break-in from a radio broadcast. But only for a second. The voice was too genuine and mysterious to be merely human. Everyone looked at the priest, as if hoping he were the sacrificial goat who could carry their sins into the desert. He stood in silence, his face white. Then he turned and left the altar.

The people were afraid to look into each other's eyes. A mother gently pushed her little girl into the aisle and walked toward the front exit. Others followed, and soon the church was empty. No one spoke. They got into their cars and drove away, each driver extremely polite to the others. And that is how it happened that there was no 10:30 Mass at St. Michael's on a bright Sunday in May.

The Our Father has been relatively easy to say until now. Though we may have only a glimmering of the depth of its meaning, we really have no problem wishing God glory, honor, the perfect fulfillment of his will, the coming of the Kingdom.

And it's not hard to ask for bread, material or spiritual—even maybe to think that we are doing our share to work for a more just distribution of the world's resources.

But now we suddenly find ourselves on trial, one hand on the Bible, the other raised to swear that we speak the truth about our Christian attitude: "Forgive us *as* we forgive."

The "as" is a stumbling block. Does it inform God that he should forgive us *because* we have already forgiven others? Because he "owes" us? Because we have put him in our debt by our admirable virtue? Not at all. We cannot create any goodness wherewith to buy the mercy or favor of God. Everything is grace, free, unearned and indiscriminate.

Does it mean "Please forgive us in the same way as we forgive others—no more, no less"? That's frightening. We want God to be divinely generous and we don't want to consider his words too closely: "In the measure that you give, it will be given you."

We're on the spot!

Let us put the second half of the petition aside for a moment. We leave the witness stand and go to the privacy of our room to be alone with God. Maybe praying the first half of the petition with full faith and sincerity will bring insight into the second half.

'Forgive Us Our Sins'

Forgive us our sins. Forgive us our debts. Forgive us our trespasses. It seems unfortunate that most of us have been saying "trespasses" all of our life. "Trespassing" is taking the shortcut over Mrs. Nitney's fine lawn, or climbing the fence and walking through Hall's woods, abundantly marked with "No Trespassing" signs. Theoretically we could be hauled up in court for a misdemeanor; but it's no big deal, actually.

In fact, it's hard to know how "trespasses" came to be the word we use today. It's not found in the Douai-Rheims version of the Bible—which was the Catholic "answer" to Protestant Bibles in 1609. It is not found in the Authorized Version—that is, the famous *King James Bible*. It was used by two of the early translators, Wycliff and Tyndale—hardly sources for Catholic usage.

Jesus was undoubtedly referring to *sin*, and the word Matthew used, say the scholars, probably preserves a Galilean word that the people readily understood as meaning "sin." Luke makes sure his Gentile readers get the fundamental message: *sin*.

In the Bible sin is the failure to achieve the aim of life. It is "missing the mark." It is the refusal to obey—concretized in the stories of Eden and Babel. It is squandering the gift of freedom. It is trying to be, *even in the face of God*, "the master of my fate...the captain of my soul."

Sometimes people come to confession and say they really have no sins. They are nice people, and they obviously don't believe that John's words apply to them: "If we say, 'We are free of the guilt of sin,' we deceive ourselves; the truth is not in us" (1 John 1:8).

Guilt. Perhaps it's because the psychologists have discovered so much *false* guilt in the modern psyche that we so easily fall into thinking that all guilt feelings are neurotic. But if we are all sinners, we are all really guilty, in one degree or another—and it is healthy and refreshing to admit it.

We needn't exaggerate our guilt; the truth is bad enough. But we must not minimize: Untruth is only more sinfulness.

> But if we acknowledge our sins,
> he who is just can be trusted
> to forgive our sins
> and cleanse us from every wrong. (1 John 1:9)

Sin is a decision, just as faith is. Perhaps it's just a little decision, today. Then it is another decision, and another. Ultimately, if this momentum is not stopped, our life is one great accumulated decision, for good or evil. In the first case, this is faith; in the second, mortal sinfulness, literally a fatal choice. There is no middle ground (unless we count those too immature to decide either way). Every decision of life moves one way or the other.

Sin and guilt are not involved in *only* this particular act or omission. If I am truly guilty of an act of slander or stealing or hate, I am still a slanderer, a thief or a hater *after* the action, until I change my basic decision.

This choice is literally for or against God, and the choice is *ongoing*. Our relationship with God is either slowly disrupted or continually built up. A relationship with God that is slowly deteriorating mirrors a relationship between husband and wife that gradually chills through selfishness. The choices go on and on, until the relationship is broken—perhaps never in actual divorce, but certainly in day-to-day reality.

Only God can give us this relationship in the first place, so we dare not think we can re-create it. We *receive* the grace of new or improved relationship. Even the first stirrings of sorrow for sinfulness are the gift of God. "Even our desire to please you is your gift," the Sacramentary says.

Our Life Is a Debt

So we stand before God as total *debtors*. We owe our very life, our every thought and decision, to him. And thus we come to that strange word Matthew uses: "Forgive us our debts."

We are total debtors *even before* we sin. Jesus, in his humanity, was absolutely and completely dependent on his Father for every breath and loving act. There is nothing that is not the gift of God.

It may be helpful to consider the "debt" we have apart from our sinning. That may not be what Jesus was talking about, but we can pray "Forgive us these debts" nevertheless.

Jesus spoke very clearly about "debts." He said, "When you have done all that is required of you, you are still unprofitable servants." A blunt truth, but ultimately refreshing: We don't have to save our own soul, because we can't.

We agree with this easily—in theory. "In him we live and move and have our being." We say, "Well, of course!" and then proceed to forget about it. After all, the evidence plainly before us is that *we* made the heroic stand against temptation; we, with admirable willpower, put down the urge to cut somebody down.

Our total dependence on God means not only that our body and soul won't continue in existence unless God continues to sustain us second by second, but that our great gift of God's life—grace—must be continually sustained also. Whatever we do, God's grace/power is there before the action.

We will never fathom the mystery of free will versus total dependence. But we can never forget the existence of either. We can't go to the extreme of quietism and say, "Well, if God does everything, let him do it," which would be as bad as thinking that we somehow save our soul, do wonderful good things, by our own power.

We stand before God—"we" including even the Mother of God—as total debtors, and it might be good for us to remember that when we pray, "Forgive us our debts," even if that meaning was not in Jesus' intention. Or was it?

'Forgive Us'

Now, if our life is a debt, how much greater is the debt of sin, when we have either destroyed the relationship of grace with God, or infected it with the sin that we love to call "venial." If we can't create the relationship in the first place, how much less can we re-create or heal it? Isn't it amazing that we take this debt so lightly?

It is one thing to be in debt to a generous friend who has enriched our life in every way; it is simply monstrous for us to violate that friend's good name by slander or ridicule.

It is easy to accept the happy debt of another's love; but it is—or should be—unthinkable that we should strike her child, or burn his crops, or desert them when they are helpless.

We can't "hurt" God, indeed. But we can hurt ourselves by insulting him. We punish our own sin by defiling our hearts. We become damaged goods, by our own choice. We carry evil within us, freely chosen. And the insult to God's precious handiwork increases as we maintain an attitude of cold pride or corrupt our mind with self-deception.

Forgive us. What does it mean? It means that by some miracle we have been able to accept the grace of God to ask for forgiveness. We may still be somewhat arrogant and unfeeling about our sin, but God has melted at least one spot in our heart.

Forgive us. If we really mean it, that is, if God has been able to create a grace-ious act in our freedom, then truth and faith take over. Truth: We are sinners, no ifs, ands or buts. Faith: God loves us anyway, always, all through our sinfulness.

Forgive us. If our plea is real, there is no cringing or groveling. We are the Prodigal Son or Daughter beginning to walk, then run, to our Father.

We say:

Forgive us the sin of our sin:
stubbornness and pride,
self-centeredness and self-sufficiency and self-seeking.
Our sin pains us
because we begin to suspect its monstrous arrogance.
But we see you as Mercy, not vindictiveness.
You are interested only in our well-being,
our total health,
our being filled with your caring.
We are running to you as your children—
sick, hobbling, weak, but running.
And as we near you, we are being made whole again.

Forgive us!
Ashamed as we are, we have a greater feeling:
We know you have forgiven us.
It would hurt you if we denied it.

'As We Forgive...'

All well and good in the moments of peace when we know we have been forgiven. God forgives easily: That's what it means to be God.

But sooner or later we realize that, although our sins are wiped away, our emotions are not. Nor are our habits. Memory cannot avoid the picture of what someone did to us, and emotion surges with memory. It *was* mean, unfair, cruel!

Habit wants to assert itself. If a horse has run free in the wide open spaces, it will be next to impossible to get a saddle on him. If a man has stopped in this bar every night on his way home, that path still beckons. If my mother only washed on sunny days, it will take her a while to break that pattern when the new electric dryer arrives.

So, after forgiveness, our fallen human nature reasserts itself as an *urge*, a *tendency*. Many people feel guilty about this, and discouraged. The sin is still there after all, they sigh.

Jesus told the adulteress that she was *forgiven*—that was the good news. He also told her to sin no more—which implied that she could, which implied that she would be tempted.

Nevertheless, the problem, not the guilt, is still there. It *is* humanly hard to forgive. Is there help available?

St. Francis once met a man he had not seen for years. The man was now penniless, and angry. When Francis asked how he was, he began cursing his master. "How should I be doing, except badly, thanks to my master, may God damn him, for he has taken everything I possess!"

Francis' reaction was one of deep compassion for the self-inflicted suffering of the poor man. He said, "Brother, forgive your master for the love of God, *so that God can free your own soul*, and perhaps he will give back what he has taken. Otherwise you will have lost your property and you will lose your soul as well." The man said, "I cannot forgive him before he has given back what he owes me." Then Francis did a typical thing: "Look, I will give you this cloak, and I beg you to forgive your master for the love of the Lord God." Francis' simple and transparent kindness softened the man, and he forgave his master.

Freedom. Even from an intelligently "selfish" point of view, even before we ever come to faith, we owe it to ourselves to free our hearts from the constricting bonds of vindictive anger, bitterness, resentment sickly nourished. Even a good pagan, a totally secular humanist, can come to the conclusion that it's not normal, not human, to allow a sick attitude to possess us—and all hate is "sick." We have all experienced this, surely—the deadness, the sourness, the misery of clinging to a vindictive spirit.

It cannot be otherwise. God made us to be like himself, and we are not "normal" when we do not love. Just as our body cannot live without bread, so our hearts cannot live without loving others—and the test of all love is forgiveness.

We have all experienced the difficulty—rather, the impossibility—of praying when we grimly hang on to our resentment. Again, it is obvious that we cannot have communion with the God who *is* mercy and love unless we allow his Spirit of mercy and love to possess us. We are slaves. We are not free.

The Anglo-Saxons Had a Word for It

Freedom is implied in the word we use so lightly: *for-give.* Ordinarily "for" means "in favor of, towards." But the old Anglo-Saxons had another meaning, which we have now lost: *completely.* To *for*-give is to give *completely, entirely, all the way.* We are called to for-give as God does—by loving completely those who hurt us—no conditions, no reservations, no subtle revenge.

The Greek word for "forgive" in the Gospels means "to send away." People who forgive *loose and let go*—a ship, an animal, a debt or an offense. "Away" is an important element in the meaning. Whatever we have a right to, whatever is due to us, we send away, we loose and let go.

Now there is no such thing as something being *half* away. Either it's gone or it isn't. What's gone in the case of forgiveness is our supposed "right" to punish someone, take revenge; our hatred, vindictiveness, desire to hurt; our demand of an eye for an eye. The one who sinned against us goes free, loose, "away." He or she is "acquitted," even though red-handedly guilty.

God sends our sins away; he gives acquittal *completely.* He looses our guilt and debt and lets it float away. He drops all charges. He resumes a relationship as if nothing had happened. Or, rather, he gives *us* the power to reenter a relationship. From God's side, nothing ever changed. He loved us the same before, during and after our sin.

The Demands of Forgiveness

Jesus, therefore, could only use his Father as a model for our forgiveness: the king who forgave an unpayable debt

(Matthew 18:23), the one who forgives endlessly, without limit (the real meaning of 70 times seven times, Matthew 18:22); and the one who says, "Offer no resistance to injury. When a person strikes you on the right cheek, turn and offer him the other. If anyone wants to go to law over your shirt, hand him your coat as well. Should anyone press you into service for one mile, go with him two miles" (Matthew 5:39-41).

Have you noticed, in the TV reporting of trial and sentencing, how avidly the family of the victim demands justice for the killer, the rapist and the kidnapper? Perfectly understandable. And they may be entirely right—perhaps the criminal should be kept out of society for life. We may sympathize totally with the family. Have you ever said, "I hope he gets the book thrown at him!"?

And yet, can we deny that when Jesus is talking about forgiveness, he is speaking to parents of children deformed by the carelessness or greed of a chemical company? To people living in filthy boxes while others ride by in Cadillacs? To a spouse who is shamed by the unfaithfulness of the other? To the mother in El Salvador whose daughter's body was sent back with the head shoved into the butchered womb? To the people who lost all their money because their bankers were thieves or gamblers? To the woman whose husband squandered her inheritance? To those who must work with or live with braggarts, hypocrites, naggers, loafers? To those who must work for unjust wages because they have no choice? To those who are the object of ridicule, discrimination, prejudice?

As the apostles said about Jesus' words promising to give them his body and blood, "This sort of talk is hard to endure! How can anyone take it seriously?" (John 6:60). The call to forgive represents a counterculture philosophy in a world where it's "obvious" that there should be an eye for an eye, and worse.

But, if loving God is the first commandment, and loving our neighbor proves our love of God, and if it's easy to love those who love us, then loving our enemies must be the touchstone that tells us whether we are Christian or not. And nothing else so confirms one of the basics of our religion: We can do nothing without the grace of God.

The demands of forgiveness are simply beyond the powers of ungraced human will. It is humanly impossible to forgive as Jesus demands. It is possible only if we accept power to do the impossible.

This includes not merely the heroic heights to which *some* rise, but the everyday 70-times-seven pardons that every Christian is called to give. It is not a humanitarian ideal, but a divine creation, one of the beautiful things only God's grace can bring to life. It is not a burden, but a privilege. We not only have the totally undeserved grace of being forgiven, but the divine ability to forgive others.

To forgive is to be like God. The reason Jesus gives for loving our enemies is that we may be children of the Father; that is, living his kind of life, loving with his kind of love. God gives the example: He makes the sun shine on the good and the bad, and sends rain upon the just and the unjust (Matthew 5:45).

God made human emotion, so he knows how it works. He knows that a father whose son has been wantonly killed is going to be *possessed* by grief and anger. He knows that the woman who worked for 30 years only to find that the bank has no money for her will suffer pain for the rest of her days. The child whose parents never showed love will suffer that rejection into adulthood.

It is not watering down Jesus' words to say that one can forgive and still feel anger and sadness and a whole gamut of other emotions. God does not demand that a widow embrace and become especially friendly with her husband's murderer. And yet she must ask herself, deep in her heart, whether or not she would help this criminal if he were in need, and she the only one who could help.

'We'—The Communal Dimension

Our discussion so far has centered on ourselves as individuals. This omits an essential part of our life and mental health—others. No one can live without the support of others (even if they are present only in memory). God, having made us, knows this, and therefore Jesus formed a *community of disciples*. We are called to show each other what it is to love and forgive. We give and request forgiveness together.

In the communal celebration of reconciliation we welcome back those who have "left" us—the community of believers. Within the supportive atmosphere of this community we are then able to forgive those who have "left" us as individuals, denying us justice and charity. As the forgiven members of God's people, the community of Jesus, we forgive others. So we pray this prayer as those who are already pardoned. In the community of brothers and sisters, we live God's life by offering and receiving love and forgiveness. Insofar as we meet the love of our brothers and sisters with our own love, God wipes out the debt they owe us, and wipes out the debt we owe them.

Once and for All

We have noted above that the Our Father is an end-time prayer in Matthew's version. That is, it presumes that Jesus will return in a relatively short time. When Jesus spoke of forgiveness he did so in the light of the coming judgment (Matthew 5:25; 6:14; 18:23; Luke 6:37).

The final pardon we hope for at the judgment seat of God is obviously not final now. We have not yet received our last and definitive absolution. The future is always at risk.

Even if, then, we no longer see the Second Coming of Jesus as imminent, we are nevertheless warned that he will come like a thief in the night. Jesus was not trying to make us into fearful eye-servers. He simply knew that today is forever. God waits, but I cannot. To postpone a wholehearted attempt at conversion is to say that I can remain somewhat estranged from God for a while.

And so, in the midst of summer sunshine, and

interesting work, in glorious health, with a perfect spouse and bright-eyed children, a paid-for house and car—I must pray as I hope to pray in my last fully conscious moments: Forgive me, set me free, once and for all, as I freely allow all anger and revenge to float away.

Father,
Abba,
free us from our slavery to anger and revenge.
Make us truly images of your Son,
free to praise you with pure hearts.
Give us your wisdom to see all others
as our brothers and sisters needing forgiveness just as we do.
Your vengeance is mercy.
Make us like you, for we are created in your image.
Help us to let loose apparent sins of others.
May we be ready to let them float away, as you are always
  ready.
We cannot love you,
we cannot be in communion with you,
if the hard shell of anger encloses us.
Free us to be human beings full of grace,
like your Son.

Matthew 6:13	*Luke 11:4*
Subject us not to the trial but deliver us from the evil one. (NAB)	and subject us not to the trial. (NAB)
And do not put us to the test, but save us from the evil one. (JB)	And do not put us to the test. (JB)
And lead us not into temptation, But deliver us from evil. (RSV)	and lead us not into temptation. (RSV)

VII

'AND LEAD US NOT INTO TEMPTATION, BUT DELIVER US FROM EVIL'

The old couple listened patiently as the discussion progressed. It had been a great retreat, a young secretary said, and heads nodded around the room. "We really need to know these beautiful things about our faith. My life isn't very exciting—and a lot of people I know have a lot of suffering. We need comfort and encouragement."

Then the old man spoke, quietly. "I don't think the Church is telling us enough about hell these days. Do we still believe there's a hell? We used to hear that anyone could actually be damned. Isn't that true anymore? Didn't Jesus give us some commandments and say that if we didn't observe them we would go to hell? Didn't he say that we have to be watchful?"

The Director of Religious Education looked at her husband and lifted her eyebrows almost imperceptibly. People coughed and looked out the window. A few smiled tolerantly.

The priest who had conducted the retreat had learned long ago that it is best to admit the validity of folks' opinions. So he said, "I guess we have toned down the old 'hell and damnation' approach because so many people were miserable, hurt, scrupulous, on edge with all the tensions of our modern life. But I have to admit that you have a point. And it's good to have people like you reminding us. The Church needs you to keep the other side 'honest.'"

This last petition of the Our Father is on the side of the "hell and damnation" people, if we follow the opinion of many scholars. But most of us breeze through the words without realizing the stern warning they contain. We need to slow down and look more closely at the meaning of this petition.

'Lead Us Not'

Let's take up the first part of the petition where we beg God *not* to lead us into temptation. The simplest answer to the seeming paradox of God's somehow cooperating in our temptations is to recall the attitude of the Hebrew mind, as evidenced throughout the Old Testament. It's an approach that we modern, science-conditioned believers find very difficult to understand. *We* know that God doesn't "send" rain—it's the result of a "high" over Whiplash, Wyoming. And God doesn't "send" the brain tumor to the nine-year-old—it came from a defect in her genes.

But, to the Jewish mind, *God did everything. God does everything.* If our side (God's people) won the war, God won it. If we lost, God caused us to lose. God raises the tides and bids the sun rise every morning. God decides that the sparrow has lived long enough, and sends the tornado that he has kept hiding in ocean mists. *Nothing* is outside God's will.

We see things the same way—but not exactly. We blame *God* for crosses, accidents, sickness and the loss of a loved one. But *we* take credit for producing color TV, laser surgery, rockets that can go to the moon and decaffeinated coffee.

Apparently here we have Jesus, *the thorough Jew*, reflecting the biblical outlook. We do, in fact, find ourselves "in temptation"; so God must lead us there, like a father putting his baby into the swimming pool and (more or less) letting him fend for himself. So what are we asking God *not* to do when we say, "Lead us not into temptation"?

We surely cannot take this petition as asking to be excused from the *normal testing* of life. God doesn't want people born into heaven with a silver spoon in their mouth. He wants people who *choose* to be his friends. Who wants "summer soldiers and sunshine patriots"? God wants people whom he can trust and who trust him—in the dark, in prison, in disgrace, in many circumstances where God seems far away. God wants us to emerge as mature people from the everyday "testing."

In this sense, temptations are moments of grace. The faithful ones stand up against the lies and cruelty of the world and speak for God. With God's grace they win the victory, and God can fill them still more with his holiness. Jesus said, generously, to his friends seated at the Last Supper, "You are the ones who have stood loyally by me in my temptations" (Luke 22:28).

God can't deliver us from the possibility of sinning unless he turns us all into robots, which wouldn't be any fun at all. God can't clap his hands and make all temptations go away, as in a fairy tale.

God couldn't put us into inevitable temptation, testing, and then have us ask him to "lead us not" into it! So what are we asking?

James, as Jewish as anybody, says,

> No one who is tempted is free to say, "I am being tempted by God." Surely God, who is beyond the grasp of evil, tempts no one. Rather the tug and lure of his own *passion* tempt every man. Once *passion* has conceived, it gives birth to sin, and when sin reaches maturity it begets death. (James 1:13-15; emphasis added)

James is saying, Don't blame God for what is your own deliberate fault. It is *this* danger "against" which we are praying.

The Real Danger

Passion conceives, sin is born, death is the grandchild. We don't need anyone to help us sin. We each have our own genius for going astray. How? By letting "passion" go unchecked.

"Passion" here means a lot more than sexual promptings. It is the *normal* urge toward the good—all good, any good. God put passion into us like voltage, powerful and exciting—but needing the proper wiring to flow through. Passion is like a flow of water in an irrigation stream. Channeled properly it produces a green field. Left to run wild, it cuts a useless gully through fertile soil.

Passion seeks the good. But sin puts created good above God. Passion puts God aside and concentrates on the obvious temporal benefit. Surely no one in all history ever said, "I *want* to sin. I *want* to break my relationship with God." Rather, the sinner averts his eyes and enjoys new friends, new wealth, new excitement.

Perhaps the greatest temptation is *success*. I will be a successful wife or husband, father or mother. I will make a success of my job, my career, my Scripture study, my work for the starving in Ethiopia. "Good" and "bad" come to mean that which contributes to or hinders my "success."

Jesus' temptations followed this path. "Give them *bread*—their minds will follow, and you'll be a successful Messiah! Give them a *show*! They'll flock to you! That's what you want, isn't it? Accept *power* from me—then you can have your way in the whole world!"

Temptation always appeals to some grand perspective, some wonder, some satisfaction. Who wants to look for a wolf under sheep's clothing?

Temptation is cumulative, like virtue. The taste of forbidden fruit stays in my memory, and we have another case of "Nothing fails like failure, nothing succeeds like success."

What we are praying then, *at least*, is:

*May no thing and no person become my god.
Help me grow strong in the normal testing of life.
Keep my eyes clear and my heart pure
as my instincts urge me toward the true and the good.*

The 'Great Trial' at the End of the World

While not denying what has just been said about the normal testing of life, a good number of responsible Scripture scholars hold that the entire Our Father, in Matthew, and especially this petition, is concerned with *the end of the world*, which in the early Church was thought to be imminent. They call it an *eschatological* prayer, that is, one that has to do with the period of the last days, the return of Christ, the destruction (in fearful battle) of the forces of evil, and the definite establishment of God's Kingdom.

The translators of the *New American Bible* have followed the scholars who say this petition refers to the *great trial*, catastrophe, battle at the end of the world, when Jesus will come and destroy the devil's power once and for all. With this context in mind the NAB uses the world *trial* where the traditional version speaks of "temptation."

The 13th chapter of Mark contains the typical (and problematic) report of the Second Coming, *combined with* an account of the destruction of Jerusalem and of the Temple. The two are hard to separate and the use of apocalyptic language (seeing a past event in the future, the use of dramatic and symbolic language) complicates the problem.

Mark concentrates on the Second Coming (the Parousia, or Presence, of Jesus) and its *nearness* and fits the terrible Jewish war, the destruction of the Temple and the suffering of Christians into preliminary signs of its coming. False Christs will arise, there will be wars and rumors of wars. But Mark says this is only the *beginning* of birth pangs. Persecution will be the lot of Christians, as the "Parousia" of Satan takes place. There will be unparalleled tribulation, and unless God shortens the days nobody will be saved. But in the terrible battle at the end Jesus will triumph, and he will save his own.

Therefore, Jesus says, be watchful. Trust. Stay faithful. I will conquer, and you will be with me:

> Because you have kept my plea to stand fast, I will keep you safe in the time of trial which is coming on the whole world, to test all men on earth. I am coming soon. (Revelation 3:10)

The last petition of the Our Father, in this "eschatological" view, is concerned with this "Great Trial" at the end. The nearer the end, the more violent the battle. The "trial" will be the final attempt of the powers of evil to gain mastery over the Kingdom of God, the people of Jesus.

We pray:

Save us from the Trial.
Protect us in those terrible days.
Do not let us be swept away.
Shorten the days.
Let us be part of your triumph!

Can anyone say this eschatological prayer today? Aren't we so sophisticated about the language-of-the-day aspect of Jesus' words that we interpret descriptions like the darkening of the sun and moon and the falling of stars in a figurative sense?

Literal or figurative, the point is the same: I myself am not finally saved. And if I go into eternity having rejected the friendship of the Father, it will be a horrendous day for me, even if the world is not drowning in fire and millions of people are not screaming in agony. Can we still dare to think of a possible "*dies irae*" for our single selves?

'Unless You Become as Little Children'

Maybe the Bomb has made us fatalists. There's nothing we can do, it seems, to prevent that monstrous evil coming through the sky in 20 minutes. So we live on the edge of doom, helpless, deliberately oblivious, pushing disaster to the back of our minds. We don't exactly eat, drink and be merry on the supposition that tomorrow we die, but we have some difficulty deciding what Christian hope really is.

And we can't help smiling when a sincere and nostalgic old couple speak about hell and damnation, commandments and sin.

Yet one of the rock-bottom truths of Christianity is that we can do nothing of ourselves. "Without me you can do nothing" is a literally true statement which could revolutionize our lives if we took it seriously. Some people may call themselves "saved," but if they are human and free they can become "unsaved." I cannot be absolutely sure I am in the state of grace, still less guarantee it for eternity.

Temptation implies the possibility of failure. Our state *is* precarious, and our life *is* a battle. We are indeed in the midst of wolves (supposing we are indeed sheep). We see cedars of Lebanon fall around us. The center does not hold.

Our greatest need today, it would seem, is to shake off a pleasant sense of security which we have put, like a veneer, over the unthinkable. We stick our heads into the sand and say that almost certainly no one would be crazy enough to blow up the world—all the while knowing any number of people who are eminently crazy enough to do it. And we rest on a sophisticated religious outlook that "demythologizes" the Scripture (an otherwise necessary task) to take all the teeth out of Jesus' warnings.

"Lead us not" is the prayer of weak people, and God help us (but of course he can't, in this case) if we don't believe it. "Lead us not" *should* mean:

*We're in danger and we're inadequate
today—and every day.
God,
Abba,
good Father,
we put ourselves into your hands.
We cannot save ourselves from death of body or spirit.
Put some steel into our flabby wills,
remove the pride of our minds.
All our virtue is your gift.
Protect us.
We're silly sheep, wayward children.*

Deliver Us From Evil—and the Evil One

Matthew's last verse (Luke omits it) has a word that can bear two meanings: "evil" in general or "the Evil One." The Church Fathers of the West generally took it to be evil in general; those of the East concentrated on a person.

Jesus spoke of the Evil One many times. He spoke of Satan (the Enemy) and of the devil (the Slanderer) and of devils. The signs he gave were of his power over evil spirits.

Unfortunately, we learned that *sometimes* "possession by the devil" in the Bible actually referred to a physical disease, such as epilepsy. All evil and sickness were thought to come from the devil, in any case. But we now are faced with the temptation to rationalize away *all* references to the devil. (If you suffer from this tendency, please read *The Screwtape Letters* by C.S. Lewis.)

The Old Testament simply assumed the existence of devils. In later Judaism they were depicted concretely, as a hierarchy led by *the* devil, Satan. In the New Testament they form a kingdom (Mark 3:22-26) opposed to God's Kingdom. They are the powers of the "world," all the "principalities and powers" that are hostile to God. They are the forces of evil. They were overcome by the cross and resurrection of Jesus, but their ultimate lack of power is not yet laid bare.

In the Bible, in Jesus' mind, the devil is *personal: the Evil One, the* Enemy. He spoke of "the Evil One" stealing away the good seed sown along the path (Matthew 13:19). Jesus prays, "I do not ask you to take them out of the world, but to guard them from the evil one" (John 17:15). He tells us, "Say yes when you mean yes and no when you mean no. Anything beyond that is from the evil one" (Matthew 5:37).

The rest of the New Testament also takes the existence of the Evil One seriously. "The Lord keeps faith; he it is who will strengthen you and guard you against the evil one" (2 Thessalonians 3:3). "We know that no one begotten of God commits sin; rather, God protects the one begotten by him, and so the evil one cannot touch him" (1 John 5:18). "Young men, I address you, for you have conquered the evil one" (1 John 2:13). "Submit to God; resist the devil and he will take flight" (James 4:7).

Perhaps we look for the devil in the wrong place. Consider how human evil operates. A dictator does not personally roust people from their homes in the dead of night. The Mafia chieftain does not personally kill those who do not cooperate. The pornographic writer does not stand on street corners hawking his wares. The man plotting to overthrow a government does not personally unpack the crates of guns. Hitler did not operate an oven at Buchenwald.

We have made the devil "cute" — Flip Wilson, or the charming bargainer in "The Devil and Daniel Webster." The devil is a character with a Van Dyke beard on lighter-fluid cans.

But the Holocaust was not the work of a "cute" and mischievous person. Surely the obscene evil of war — especially the kind we now face — is more malicious than its human perpetrators can understand. The greedy possession of most of the riches of the earth by a relative few is not the work of a few entrepreneurs. The literal slavery of millions of human beings is unhuman in the worst sense. Human beings must be cooperators, guilty but not totally comprehending. The efficient slaughter of millions of unborn human beings is humanly mind-boggling. There must be something monstrously evil at work.

Pope John Paul II has recently reminded us of the "mystery of iniquity" and of what he calls, in a striking phrase, "the communion of sin." God created a solidarity among human beings—the communion of saints, of holy things. Thanks to this, it is possible to say that whenever we rise above ourselves we raise the world. But to this mystery of divine love there is opposed the "mystery of iniquity" of which Paul speaks with reference to the Antichrist (2 Thessalonians 2:7). Allied to this is the reality of a "communion of sin," "whereby a soul that lowers itself through sin drags down with itself the Church and, in some way, the whole world" (*Apostolic Exhortation on Reconciliation and Penance*, 16).

In the same document, the Pope says, "Clearly sin is the product of man's freedom. But deep within its human reality there are factors at work which place it beyond the merely human, in the border area where man's conscience, will and sensitivity are in contact with the dark forces of evil which, according to St. Paul, are active in the world almost to the point of ruling it" (14).

It is possible, in the face of all this, to pray for deliverance from "evil in general," which could include the Evil One. But the force of the prayer would seem to be lost. Besides, those familiar with the biblical languages remind us that the prayer actually says "*the* Evil One"; when "evil in general" is meant, the New Testament has "all evil."

How much more realistic to think of a *person* when Jesus says, referring to the accusation that he cast out devils by the power of Beelzebub, prince of devils: "When a strong man fully armed guards his courtyard, his possessions go undisturbed. But when someone stronger than he comes and overpowers him, such a one carries off the arms on which he was relying and divides the spoils" (Luke 11:21-22).

Christians have the promise that they will be protected from the Evil One. "God protects the one begotten by him, and so the evil one cannot touch him. We know that we belong to God, while the whole world is under the evil one" (1 John 5:18-19). This "world" is not God's good world and people, but the apparently invincible kingdom of Satan. This prayer says we need to be "snatched" from the Evil One.

The final great strengthening *certainty* we have is that we already have with us the Jesus who will save us from the Trial, from temptation, from evil, from the Evil One. The One who taught the prayer answers it:

Father,
save us from the Evil One,
and from all the powers of evil.
Help us to see evil in all its forms,
especially in the deceptions of the Father of Lies.
Your power is in us;
your Spirit is with us.
You live in us;
we are the brothers and sisters of Jesus.
We cannot be conquered when we keep our eyes on you,
our hearts filled with your strength,
and our hands reaching out to help others.
We trust your love,
now and at the hour of our death.

VIII

'For Thine Is the Kingdom and the Power and the Glory Forever and Ever. Amen.'

This doxology, or praise of God, was used by the Jews at the time of Christ. Some Christians added it to the Our Father early on, as can be seen from the version of the prayer in the *Didache* (*The Teaching of the Apostles*), which was written before 100 A.D.

It is found in some manuscripts of the New Testament, but not in the best ones. It has never been included in any Catholic translation. Protestants know it from the *King James Bible*, though it has been moved to a footnote in the *Revised Standard Version* of the same. One scholar says, "It is sheer accident that it did not appear in the Greek manuscripts that Jerome used in translating the Vulgate."

Wherever it came from, the Catholic Church has incorporated it into the Mass, after the prayer "Deliver us" which follows the Our Father. An example of "in nonessentials, liberty."

Conclusion

The food of Jesus' mortal life was to do what "Abba" willed, to please "Abba," to be a child with his hand in "Abba's" hand. Because this love burned within him, he could be the adult son who took responsibility for the whole world, and faced death down with the terrible power of his holiness.

Perhaps the greatest lesson most of us have to learn is to pray the Our Father more in Jesus' spirit. And, first of all, that means paying greater attention to the first half of the prayer: *God is first. God is all.*

Our concerns weigh upon us, understandably—food, forgiveness, safety. And "Abba" listens kindly. But we must grow up too, and see the full picture. The one fact of life before all others simply is: God is love. God be praised. God be blessed. God be thanked. God *be*.

Second, we might pay more attention to the "end-time" emphasis of Matthew's version. No one should sit back and wait for the end, of course. Paul condemned that attitude in his Thessalonian parish long ago. Still, it seems good to stand back from our lives, once in a while, and realize that we are living only an infinitesimal part of our eternal existence. It is not a "pie in the sky" mentality to face a simple truth: God's total "success" is not yet accomplished. Can we sympathize at all with the almost-last words of the Bible: "Come, Lord Jesus"?

Father Raymond Brown describes how Matthew's community of the first century, anxiously expecting the Second Coming, prayed the Our Father. Note the finality in some words:

> ...that God will completely glorify His name by establishing His kingdom, which represents the fulfillment of the plan He has willed for both earth and heaven. For its portion in this consummation of time, the community asks a place at the heavenly banquet table to break bread with Christ, and a forgiveness of its sins. A titanic struggle with Satan stands between the community and the realization of its prayer, and from this it asks to be delivered.

Finally, some words from an expert to reassure us that the Our Father is always "good-enough" prayer. St. Teresa of Avila, one of the great lights in the history of prayer, tells this story in her *Way of Perfection*:

> I know a nun who could never practice anything but vocal prayer....She came to me in great distress, saying that she did not know how to practice mental prayer, and that she could not contemplate but could only say vocal prayers. She was quite an old woman and had lived an extremely good and religious life. I asked her what prayers she said, and from her reply I saw that, though keeping to the *Our Father*, she was experiencing pure contemplation, and the Lord was raising her to be with him in union....So I praised the Lord and envied her her vocal prayer.

As the tempo of our lives speeds up, our prayer must slow down — even to two words: "Abba, Father!" We need make no apologies if this prayer is "all" that we say. It is the Lord's prayer, and he delights to hear us say it.
Slowly.